Polling On The Issues

The edited proceedings of a conference
sponsored by the National Council on Public
Polls and the Charles F. Kettering Foundation,
Washington, D.C., November 1979.

KJ A REPORT
FROM THE KETTERING FOUNDATION

Polling On The Issues

Edited by
ALBERT H. CANTRIL
President
National Council on Public Polls

SEVEN LOCKS PRESS
Cabin John, Md./Washington, D.C.

Copyright © 1980 by the Charles F. Kettering Foundation

Library of Congress Cataloging in Publication Data

Polling on the issues.
   "The edited proceedings of a conference sponsored by the National Council
on Public Polls and the Charles F. Kettering Foundation, Washington, D.C.,
November 1979."

   "A report from the Charles F. Kettering Foundation."
   1. Public opinion polls.   I. Cantril, Albert Hadley, 1940— II. National
Council on Public Polls (United States) III. Charles F. Kettering Foundation.
HM261.P575   303.3'8   80-23439

ISBN 0-932020-02-X
ISBN 0-932020-03-8 (pbk.)

Manufactured in the United States of America

SEVEN LOCKS PRESS
P.O. Box 72
Cabin John, Md. 20731

Preface

PUBLIC OPINION POLLS have become so pervasive in our society that a fresh look at their methods, interpretation, and use is most timely.

Too often public opinion polls are treated as ends in themselves—a form of gossip half-accepted as gospel—rather than useful tools for probing the complexity of public images, attitudes, and behavior. People love polls; everyone can quote the latest poll relating to his or her particular interest—and most of the time the polls people cite support their own preconceived opinions. And because people love polls, the media love them too. While everyone has access to many polls, too few people seem to know what to do with them.

The concern of the Charles F. Kettering Foundation about public opinion research is long-standing. Our experience with polling began in 1966, when we first used surveys in our efforts to improve elementary and secondary education. We felt then, as now, that it is not enough to develop new programs; we needed to find out how the programs could gain greater acceptance by the public and the policymakers, the school boards. We saw a need to upgrade education from two perspectives, combining a research and development "push" with a policy "pull."

Our original concerns about linking polling to policy have been broadened and reinforced by subsequent experience in other policy areas. In 1976 and 1977 we sponsored a series of metropolitan opinion polls on foreign policy in connection with "town meetings" between citizens and State Department officials. These meetings were sponsored by local world affairs councils, and the accompanying surveys were conducted or arranged by the Communications Research Center of Cleveland State University. The poll results were introduced into meetings so that the views of the "man in the street" would not be overlooked during discussions between local leaders and officials from the State Department. They were an eye-opener for our staff as well as for participating officials.

One memorandum to the Secretary of State said: "The most striking—indeed disturbing—general impression with which we return is that [often citizens] do not understand many of the bedrock principles on which our foreign policy is based. In part, this reflects the growing complexity (even ambiguity) of our international relationships. . . ."

The complexity and ambiguity of international relations in an imploding world—a world dramatically bursting inward on itself—were illuminated by an extraordinary survey on human needs and satisfactions conceived by George Gallup and carried out in 1974-75 by Gallup International research institutes in cooperation with the Kettering Foundation. This survey sampled opinion in 60 countries representing nearly two-thirds of the world's population. As Dr. Gallup reported in the *Reader's Digest*, "The fact that dominates the survey is the economic gulf that separates the 'have' from the 'have not' nations."

Domestically, we joined with the Mott Foundation in 1977 to sponsor an urban poll by The Gallup Organization, seeking to discover what city residents really think about American cities—what prompts many to leave, and what would entice them to stay.

The conference upon which this book is based examined the complex set of relationships among the public, pollsters, reporters, interpreters, and policymakers. It is our hope that this volume will help direct the growing philosophical and methodological concerns relating to opinion research to a research agenda that will chart a course for greater polling depth and precision, make interpretation more trenchant, and shed more light on the trade-off issues that are the sport and torment of politicians and policy planners.

PHILLIPS B. RUOPP
VICE PRESIDENT, SOCIAL SCIENCES
CHARLES F. KETTERING FOUNDATION

Contents

POLLING ON THE ISSUES

Contributors

PATRICK H. CADDELL is president of Cambridge Survey Research, Inc. and president of Cambridge Reports, Inc.

ALBERT H. CANTRIL is president of Cantril Research, Inc. and president of the National Council on Public Polls. He has served on the White House staff, the Bureau of the Budget and the Department of State. Among his publications are *POLLS: Their Use and Misuse in Politics* and *Hopes and Fears of the American People.*

IRVING CRESPI is vice president of The Roper Organization Inc. A former senior fellow at Mathematica Policy Research and executive vice president of The Gallup Organization, he is a past president of the American Association for Public Opinion Research (AAPOR) and the World Association for Public Opinion Research.

JAMES FALLOWS is Washington Editor for the *Atlantic Monthly*. Before serving as chief speech writer for President Jimmy Carter, he was contributing editor to the *Washington Monthly*.

MERVIN D. FIELD is director of The Field Institute's California Poll and chairman of The Field Research Corporation. He has held numerous offices in the American Association for Public Opinion Research and has received its AAPOR Award. He is a trustee of the National Council on Public Polls.

GEORGE H. GALLUP is founder of The Gallup Poll and chairman of The Gallup Organization. He has received the AAPOR Award and has served as president of the National Muncipal League, as a trustee of the Charles F. Kettering Foundation, and is currently a trustee of the National Council on Public Polls. He is author of many books, including *The Sophisticated Poll Watcher's Guide.*

LEONARD GARMENT is a partner in the law firm of Mudge Rose Guthrie and Alexander. He served as a Special Consultant to President Richard Nixon until 1973 with particular responsibilities in domestic policy.

JACK W. GERMOND writes a nationally syndicated political column with Jules Witcover for the *Washington Star.* He has been a political columnist for the paper since 1974. Earlier he served as Washington bureau chief for the Gannett News Service.

PETER D. HART is president of Peter D. Hart Research Associates, Inc. He is a consultant to CBS News and is a Woodrow Wilson Visiting Fellow of The Woodrow Wilson National Fellowship Foundation.

ROBERT B. HILL is Director of Research for the National Urban League. He was formerly associated with the Bureau of Applied Social Research at Columbia University. He is author of *Strengths of Black Families.*

SUSAN B. KING is chairman of the Consumer Product Safety Commission. She has served as Washington director for the National Committee for an Effective Congress and as director of the Center for Public Financing of Elections.

EVERETT CARLL LADD, JR. is professor of political science, director of the Institute for Social Inquiry and executive director of The Roper Center at the University of Connecticut. Among his books are *American Political Parties: Transformations of the American Party System* and *Where Have All the Voters Gone?*

WILLIAM J. LANOUETTE is a staff correspondent for the *National Journal* specializing in national security issues and nuclear energy. He has covered the Strategic Arms Limitation Talks since 1969, first for the *National Observer* and, since 1977, for the *National Journal*. Earlier he was a researcher/reporter for *Newsweek* and a congressional aide.

ROBERT CAMERON MITCHELL, a sociologist, is a senior fellow at Resources for the Future, a private non-profit research organization in Washington, D.C. His research interests include public opinion on environmental and energy issues. Among his publications is "Silent Spring/ Solid Majorities" in *Public Opinion* magazine.

WARREN J. MITOFSKY is director of the Election and Survey Unit of CBS News. He established the CBS/New York Times Poll and designed the election analysis system used by the network since 1967. Before joining CBS he was chief of the Special Surveys Branch of the Bureau of the Census. He is a trustee of the National Council on Public Polls and chairman of its Committee on Disclosure.

HARRY W. O'NEILL is executive vice president and a director of the Opinion Research Corporation. He has been active in the Council of American Survey Research Organizations.

He is treasurer and a former trustee of the National Council on Public Polls.

ITHIEL DE SOLA POOL is professor of political science at the Massachusetts Institute of Technology. He is a former director of the Simulmatics Corporation and member of the Defense Science Board. Among his publications is *Candidates, Issues and Strategies.*

BURNS W. ROPER is chairman of The Roper Organization Inc. and chairman of The Roper Center at the University of Connecticut (Storrs). A former president of the Market Research Council, he is active in the American Association for Public Opinion Research. He is a trustee and former vice president of the National Council on Public Polls.

PHILLIPS B. RUOPP is vice president for the social sciences of the Charles F. Kettering Foundation.

BARRY SUSSMAN is editor for polls and special projects at the *Washington Post.* Prior to his involvement with the Washington Post Poll, he served as special editor for the *Washington Post's* coverage of Watergate. He is author of *The Great Cover-Up: Nixon and the Scandal of Watergate.*

PAUL C. WARNKE is a partner in the law firm of Clifford and Warnke. He is former director of the U.S. Arms Control and Disarmament Agency. In this capacity he was the principal U.S. negotiator on the second Strategic Arms Limitation Treaty. During the Johnson Administration he served as Assistant Secretary of Defense for International Security Affairs.

MARTIN WEINBERGER is a senior vice president of Oxtoby-Smith Inc., a New York market research firm. He joined Oxtoby-Smith as director of research in 1962.

Polling On The Issues

Introduction

PART OF THE GENIUS of the American political process is the diversity of individuals and institutions that serve as brokers between public opinion and decision makers.

Sometimes the mediation of public sentiment takes place through the formal structures of our representative system. Other times it occurs through the less formal, *ad hoc* advocacy of particular points of view. Whatever mix may exist from time to time between the more and less formal approaches, the public opinion poll has emerged pre-eminent as a vehicle for characterizing the public's view of "the public interest." Since the inception of modern survey techniques in the mid-30s, the polls have been an increasing part of the political calculus through which public policy develops.

Of the many kinds of information consumed in the decision-making process, that provided by the polls is unique in two important respects. First, poll findings are often heralded as having an ability to sort through the ambiguities inherent in most political issues and yield incisive insights. Second, poll findings contribute that most precious form of political intelligence: a basis for anticipating the probable consequences of one decision or another.

3

POLLING ON THE ISSUES

In recent years polling has become so pervasive a force in the political process as to warrant an inquiry into its impact, both intended and unintended, on the environment within which decisions are made and public policies evolve. Such an inquiry should attempt to bring to bear the perspectives of three relevant parties:

- Pollsters, including those who are academically based, who are generally confident of their ability to measure and interpret public opinion and its underlying dynamic;
- Journalists, who have a clear sense of when and how information about public opinion becomes newsworthy;
- Decision makers, who have varying views about when public opinion becomes crucial as policies affecting the public are shaped.

On November 8, 1979, at the invitation of the National Council on Public Polls and the Charles F. Kettering Foundation, more than a hundred guests from these three constituencies convened in the conference room of the Washington Post building to hear presentations and exchange views about "Polling on the Issues."

The conference grew out of the two sponsors' converging interests. The National Council on Public Polls is an association of public opinion research organizations concerned about the quality of opinion polls and their reporting by the print and broadcast media. Founded in 1969, the National Council has been working for higher standards in the field of public opinion research and for greater understanding of polls and polling techniques by journalists, decision makers, and the general public.

The Charles F. Kettering Foundation has long been active in the support of public opinion research. The Foundation has focused increasingly on the adequacy of polling as a technique for assessing the state of public thinking and on the role of the polls in the policy process.

During the conference no attempt was made to reach a consensus on the issues discussed. Rather, the purpose of the conference was to highlight the more important considerations involved in "polling on the issues" growing out of the experience of both producers and consumers of polls.

This book presents the edited proceedings of the conference. Some of the presentations were prepared formally and with an eye toward their subsequent inclusion in this volume. Others, including the comments of discussants, were more extemporaneous. The resulting variations in style have been preserved in order to reflect the flow of each participant's contribution.

The organization of the book follows that of the conference: one section for each of the four panels. Discussion from the floor followed each panel; highlights from the discussion are included at the end of each section.

Polling:
Journalism or Social Science?
(Panel I)

The relationship between polling and journalism, the subject of the first panel, can be traced to the earliest days of public opinion research. From the outset journalism was looked to as a safe haven that would protect polling from political influences and insure its independence and objectivity.

Over the years, however, polling and journalism have grown increasingly interdependent. Much of polling today is either supported by the print and broadcast media through syndication of poll reports to media subscribers or actually conducted by news organizations that have established their own polls. In addition, members of the press corps turn with growing frequency to pollsters and poll findings for leads around which to organize stories.

Indeed, many stories are based on poll findings alone.

Both institutions have been affected. On the one hand, journalism has left its mark on both the kinds of polls that are conducted and the way poll results are interpreted and reported. This has been a function of values essential to journalism: an emphasis on speed in dealing with "perishable" material; a need to distill complex material into concise and readily comprehensible form; and a focus on the topical and immediate significance of developments. Increasing controversy has resulted over what information about a poll should be highlighted by journalists in order to provide the public with an adequate basis for assessing the validity of a reported poll result.

On the other hand, public opinion research has had a significant impact on journalism. A kind of "news" is created through polls that would not otherwise exist. This "news" usually has political implications that in turn influence developments later reported. Even the political reporter's work has been affected by the degree to which polls and poll findings penetrate the specific situations that are being covered—and the way they are covered. Further, news organizations now conducting polls of their own are often called upon to defend themselves against the contention that they have a vested interest in reporting their own taking of the public pulse or that they give short shrift to "news" from competitors' polls.

From either profession's perspective, the problem persists of establishing a balance between journalistic criteria of what is "newsworthy" and research criteria of what constitutes a valid measure of public opinion. The focal question addressed by the first panel at the conference was therefore:

> Given the proximity of polling to journalism, what are the implications of the tensions between the process of measuring public opinion, on the one hand, and the requirements and constraints of journalism, on the other?

Issues Into Percentages
(Panel II)

The reported percentages of a public opinion poll do not necessarily constitute public opinion. They are nothing more than the frequency with which a sample of respondents gives varying answers to specific questions asked. Assuming technical proficiency in sampling and field work, widely disparate findings may emerge from different polls on a common issue due to the way questions are phrased, the sequence in which questions are asked, and other dimensions of what the statistician refers to as "non-sampling error" in surveys. It is this facet of polling that draws on the art in the "art-science" of opinion research.

The proliferation of polling in recent years has increased the chances that simultaneous measures of opinion will yield conflicting assessments. Each word or phrase in a poll question can introduce a nuance that affects the dimension of sentiment tapped. The direction of an individual's leaning on a particular subject, for example, may be of varying importance depending on the intensity of feelings, the amount of information a respondent has on the subject at hand, or the specificity and clarity of the question.

Polling on public policy issues presents a particular challenge in this respect. The danger always exists of conveying a clear division of opinion on an issue when the public's attitudes may not have crystallized or when they have taken shape along other dimensions than those suggested by the pollster's questioning. The opinion analyst's challenge is to characterize as accurately as possible the full range of the public's views on a subject. This necessarily involves superimposing a set of assumptions about the pertinent dimensions of opinion and the categories within which it is to be measured. Therein lies the chance that the questions asked, and thus the resulting percentages, may be more artifacts of the analyst's terms of reference than an indication of what is truly at work in the public's thinking.

The problem is compounded by the tensions alluded to earlier between the different habits of thought and objectives of the journalist and the social scientist. Add to these the needs of decision-makers for information about opinion in terms that are perceived by them to be relevant to policy, and the mix of nuances in issue polling becomes imposing.

Even with painstakingly balanced measurement of opinion, it remains for the analyst to attribute significance to the findings. Public opinion often appears inconsistent and contradictory. Sometimes this is the genuine state of public thinking on an issue—particularly one about which people may be ill-informed. At other times the conflicting findings are an indication that the opinion analyst has not yet unearthed the forces embodied in public opinion on the issue. In still other instances analysts may simply differ in their interpretation of a common set of data.

Accordingly, the focal question asked the second panel:

> How can public opinion on policy issues be most adequately measured and interpreted, particularly when many issues are complex and likely to be remote from the daily concerns of the public?

The Impact of the Polls on the Policy Environment (Panel III)

Not long after leaving his unique vantage point in Lyndon Johnson's White House, Bill Moyers wrote: "When policies and laws outdistance public opinion, or take public opinion for granted, or fail to command respect in the conscience of the people, they lose their 'natural' legitimacy."*

---

* "One Thing We Learned," *Foreign Affairs* (July, 1968), pp. 661-662.

Modern polling has lent an especially contemporary quality to this age-old question of democracy: how and when should public opinion be taken into account in the making of decisions? Some feel that polls should be consulted only to guide the implementation of a policy and its presentation to the public; others feel they should be looked to for guidance in shaping an overall policy; and still others feel it is not possible to pose a sharp distinction between the means and ends of public policy.

At the operational level politicians need two basic kinds of information about public opinion: (a) the extent to which it has crystallized on a given issue; and (b) the factors that account for the inconsistencies so often manifest in the public's perception of an issue. This kind of information requires the opinion analyst's assessment of many variables, including the public's knowledge on an issue, the extent to which events have been assimilated by the public, the degree to which people feel they have a personal stake in the matter at hand, and the underlying context within which the issue is viewed by the public.

The task of providing this kind of information is subject to the exigencies of the policy formulation process in two respects. First, decisions often need to be made quickly, resulting in the requirement that the right information get to the right individual at the right time. This requirement affects the institutional and structural relationship between opinion analyst and decision maker. A variety of models exists: a private pollster whose principal client is the president; the survey organization responding to government research needs; and the staff within an executive or legislative branch office responsible for the analysis of public opinion.

A second consideration is the frequent complaint about oversimplification of issues in poll questions. This problem must itself be seen as part of the larger issue of how to formulate poll questions that are truly relevant to the concerns of policy-makers without asking for opinions where none exist or producing misleading results by phrasing questions in terms that do not capture respondents' attitudes.

As a complement to the opinion researcher's perspective on these matters, the third panel of the conference brought together individuals with substantial and diverse experience at the policy level. They addressed two questions:

> Of what consequence are public opinion polls in terms of their effect on public policy?

> What are the requirements for public opinion polls to contribute, if at all, to better public policy?

Polling:
A Political Institution?
(Panel IV)

As part of the larger question of the role and competence of public opinion, modern polling raises anew the question of balancing majority consensus with the rights of the minority. Polling has a unique ability to place the contending claims of special interests in the broader context of the commonweal.

Pollsters take unto themselves an immense public trust when they report the state of public thinking. Polls can have considerable consequence in their ever-present reporting of majority and minority views on the issues. As the print and broadcast media become more heavily involved in their own polling, increasingly the public's voice is heard through the distribution curves of public opinion researchers. Not only are these distribution curves only as valid as the technical proficiency of a poll, they are also dependent on the way a given issue has been formulated by the analyst.

Special interests themselves have a voracious appetite for poll results. They constitute probably the largest single client group for polling firms and make active use of survey results in advancing their causes. No serious doubt is raised about the legitimate right of a single interest to commission a private poll. The issue is joined, however, when poll results are used for purposes of promoting a particular point of view. Diverse attitudes exist within the field of opinion research about the appropriate posture for the opinion analyst in wrestling with the seeming incompatibility of objectivity and advocacy.

While polls can help put the protestations of varying interests into a larger perspective, they can be flawed by their failure to represent the nuances in the concerns of groups that are minorities in a demographic sense (such as a particular regional, age or racial group) but which are not monolithic in their views on particular issues. By over-sampling specific population subgroups, pollsters can help overcome this deficiency; but it is inherent in the sampling concept that numerical minorities tend to be submerged in overall national poll results.

Disparities in poll findings acquire increasing significance as polls become more visible components of the national debate on policy issues. The results of both public and private polls surface frequently in the national media, the hearings of congressional committees, pleadings before regulatory agencies, and promotional campaigns for one cause or another.

Each time poll figures differ, a clamor may arise as journalists and issue proponents call for explanation of the discrepancy. The immediate political aspects of these differences in findings, however, are less important than the larger matter of how public opinion polling is ultimately held accountable. Although individual polling firms are often understandably defensive about their own findings, most professional survey organizations concur in the belief that publicly released poll findings, whether contested or not, should be able to withstand public scrutiny. Even so, the practicalities of institutionalizing such scrutiny are complex.

The fourth panel at the conference was asked to address this cluster of issues. The focal question was:

> Have the polls become a political institution in their own right and, if so, what are the implications for the future of polling and its relationship to journalism and the policy process?

Editorial Perspective

A brief word is due about the editorial judgments that have guided preparation of this volume. As noted earlier, the individual presentations have not been edited into a uniform style. Conference proceedings such as these present the dilemma of how to impose a format without compromising the unique flavor of the individual contributions. The questions and discussion from the floor following each panel are included and have been edited solely to reflect the general flow of the give-and-take.

This volume contains no concluding "summary" chapter, for such a chapter would have required the editor to highlight some points over others and to draw the more important implications of points made. Some readers, therefore, might find this volume wanting for the lack of a final word. Since no attempt was made at the conference to achieve a convergence of judgment among participants, it was our judgment that to do so here would be inappropriate.

Finally, the responsibility for the presentations herein rests with the individual contributors and not with their affiliate institutions, the Charles F. Kettering Foundation, or the National Council on Public Polls.

ALBERT H. CANTRIL
PRESIDENT, NATIONAL COUNCIL
ON PUBLIC POLLS
CONFERENCE CHAIRMAN

PART I

Polling: Journalism or Social Science?

Given the proximity of polling to journalism, what are the implications of the tensions between the process of measuring public opinion, on the one hand, and the requirements and constraints of journalism, on the other?

The first conference panel began by addressing this question from two perspectives: a pollster's assessment of the impact of journalism on polling and a journalist's assessment of polling's impact on journalism. Burns W. Roper and Jack W. Germond are both highly regarded in their own spheres of expertise and each has a more than fleeting acquaintance with the other's trade. Their presentations highlight, therefore, the general elements of the tension between polling and journalism.

To illustrate the competing influences at work on the pollster, Irving Crespi then examines a prominent aspect of opinion polling—measurements of presidential popularity. Through the specific focus on popularity polling, Crespi documents the genesis of such polling in the interface between journalism and opinion research, its subsequent development, and the profound impact such polling has on our political process.

Two discussants then review the Roper, Germond, and Crespi presentations from different vantage points. Ithiel de Sola Pool is a political scientist sensitive to the nuances of

POLLING ON THE ISSUES

American politics, and knowledgeable about polling in particular and political communications in general. His remarks are complemented by those of Barry Sussman, a journalist who combines the two areas of expertise central to the panel's discussion: opinion research and editorial responsibilities at a major newspaper.

AHC

14

Burns W. Roper

The Impact of Journalism on Polling

FROM THE PERSPECTIVE of a pollster rather than a journalist, journalism has ten significant effects on polling—eight negative and two positive. This does not mean, however, that the effects of journalism on polling have been four times as bad as they have been good.

Let me jump right into the effects. (1) The initial impact of journalism on polling was to hold polling back, to retard its growth. Newsmen initially saw polling as competitive, as an invasion of the newsman's function and prerogatives. As a result, the news media avoided publishing or airing poll results as much as possible—with the result that polls did not achieve the visibility that they now have, and that I think they deserved back in the '30s, '40s, and '50s.

(2) On those occasions when the news media *did* report poll results, they showed little critical judgment or discrimination about what they reported. They had little understanding of polling, or what constituted good polling, and they tended to give the bad at least equal weight with the good. I remember a situation in the '60s in which a major newspaper reported the results of an Ohio congressman's mail poll of his constituents as a page one story in the Sunday edition; buried at the bottom of about page 35 was a four-inch summation of a Gallup poll on exactly the same subject showing opposite results. The level of sophistication of this paper—by no means unique at the time—was such that they apparently assumed that 4,000 returns from a mail survey in a congressman's district were superior to a 1,500 national sample—even though the 4,000 represented about a two percent return on the congressman's poll.

For reasons I can't fully explain, the media became

converts to polls early in the 1970s. Many of them even set up their own survey units, which brings me to the next point.

(3) The media converts made a mistake, in my judgment, in sending a bright newsman to a two- or six-week course on polling techniques and then establishing him as their survey expert. They have installed promising trainees where they should have experienced veterans. This is not said in criticism of the individuals involved. To illustrate what I mean, turn it around the other way. I would not be at all offended if Jack Germond did not think I could be city editor of the *Washington Star* after a two-week training course; nor would I be at all offended if Barry Sussman didn't think I could be a *Washington Post* bureau chief after six weeks of training.

(4) Partly because of their lack of deep expertise, the media have overstressed sampling error and understressed the more important and considerably greater sources of error. And in the process of stressing sampling error, they have not warned the reader or viewer of error as they have intended. Instead, they have implied an unwarranted degree of accuracy. They have, in effect, said: "This finding is within three percentage points of what the entire American public thinks on this subject," when, in fact, a differently worded question might—and often does—produce a result that is 25 or 30 points different from the reported result.

(5) Historically, the media have dealt with what others have said or done. They have reported or over-reported or under-reported or not reported at all what was said or done, but it was what *others* said or did that was their concern. Now that they have gotten into the polling business, they have changed their function. They are now in the position of *making* news, not merely reporting it, and I think this presents them with some problems.

(6) As a result of having their own polls, the media have a natural inclination to push their own polls. NBC is not eager to devote the same attention to the Gallup Poll that it

devotes to the NBC/Associated Press Poll. Nor does it feature the CBS/New York Times Poll as prominently as CBS does. This is particularly true when the results of another poll conflict with and raise doubts about the sponsoring medium's own poll. You don't often hear, "Yesterday we reported that our poll showed X; a Gallup Poll released today casts serious doubt on the validity of that finding."

(7) The news media have put an unwarranted premium on speed. In their view, any poll result that is more than four days old isn't worth reporting. A quick reading, with a hastily drawn questionnaire, using a telephone sample, is far more significant to the average news medium than is a personal interview survey, with a carefully drawn questionnaire, administered after the dust has settled. And, because speed is important, it is often the initial or first reaction that is tapped, not the public's considered judgment.

(8) Related to this speed consideration, but also partly a function of the telephone interview method, complex issues tend to be dealt with in oversimplified questions that are designed not to exceed 10 to 15 words.

(9) On the positive side, the emphasis the news media put on speed has resulted not only in the news media polls being processed and reported fast, but in some of the non-media polls being reported faster as well. In the last couple of months, for example, we have cut a full two weeks out of our processing and reporting schedule. This is quite frankly a response to the fact that if a poll is more than four days old, the news media see little utility in it.

(10) The pendulum swing from media resistance to polls to media embracing of polls has created a broad awareness and acceptance of polling which it would not have otherwise. If the media held back polling in the earlier days, they have more than made up for it in the last few years. By their conversion to polls, the media have given the public a louder voice than it has had heretofore.

Points (1) and (2) are now unimportant because they are water over the dam; the media are no longer inhibiting the acceptance of polling—quite the contrary. And as the media have gotten more interested in polls, they have become better informed about them and more discriminating as between good and bad polls. Point (3) will take care of itself as the bright young men with two to six weeks of training become seasoned veterans. When this happens, the over-stressing of sampling error and understressing of other sources of error will probably disappear, as will the emphasis on speed and the use of simplistic questions to measure first top-of-the-head reaction.

It is my points (5) and (6) that I continue to be concerned about. I think the media, those that have their own polls at least, have not only a full disclosure problem but a conflict-of-interest problem. The broadcast media almost never tell the listeners what the question they asked was, reporting only their conclusion and the percentage result from an unknown question. All too often the print media also do not reveal the question they have asked—again, just the percentage and the conclusion they draw. This practice leaves the listener or reader with no way of evaluating a result. One approach would be always to include the question wording—in my judgment, a far better use of time and space than the wholly misleading plus-or-minus three percent error statement. The media contend that they don't have the time or space to devote to question wording; but somehow they always manage to find the time and space to assure readers and listeners that they can count on these results to within plus-or-minus three percentage points. An alternative to revealing the question asked would be to devote equal time or space to the results of a reputable poll showing different or contrary results from the media's own polls.

It seems to me that the problems of disclosure and conflict of interest are serious for those media who have their own polls. If and when they can find an effective way of dealing with those problems, the two positive effects I have cited will more than offset the eight negatives I have cited. Several of those negatives are water over the dam already; others I feel sure will disappear with time. If these two remaining negatives can be dealt with, the effects of journalism on polling will become entirely positive.

Jack W. Germond

The Impact of Polling on Journalism

I HAVE APPEARED so often on these panels carping about the way newspapers and broadcast stations use public opinion polls that I am in danger of becoming a public scold. The one thing I have learned from this experience is that it is necessary to make some disclaimers at the outset, although I have little confidence they will not be largely forgotten or ignored after the fact.

The first is simply that I don't represent myself to be a critic of the way opinion research is conducted. That is not my area of expertise, and I have a great deal of respect for and faith in the Peter Harts and Bob Teeters of this world. I've learned repeatedly that the polls are generally accurate measures of a situation at the time they are taken.

Second, I don't quarrel with anyone's right to take the temperature of the masses every hour on the hour, however much I may be convinced they are simply quantifying the obvious, however much I may be convinced that much of the data can serve no conceivable purpose, useful or otherwise. If some pollster wants to find out how many baldheaded men under 50 prefer scotch to bourbon, that is his affair. Just don't ask me to get very interested or, worse yet, to print it in my newspaper.

Third—and this is the most important caveat, I suspect— I don't deny that I rely on polling data all the time. As a reporter I devour it, to the point that it has become a necessity for me in covering many campaigns. For example, I just finished doing a series of columns about some of the 1979 mayoral and gubernatorial campaigns, and the polling data in all cases were extraordinarily accurate. As a result of that polling, my columns were much more impressive than they otherwise would have been. Even when I don't think it is worth putting in the paper, I also like to know something about Alan Cranston's approval rating in California or how the labor vote is splitting on Carter and Kennedy in Ohio. Beyond that, I often find insights in public opinion research that are simply not available to me from any other source.

My point then—and this is the difficult distinction to make—is that I am not a critic of polls, or at least not of most of them. What I find abominable is the way newspapers use them as a substitute for, rather than supplement to, the kind of thorough political reporting that is far more meaningful and, not incidentally, interesting. (Although I will refer to newspapers largely, I am talking about both newspapers and broadcast media. Most of the sins of the newspapers, I think, are compounded by broadcast media. They are even less responsible and sophisticated in handling the material than we are.)

The explosion in the number of polls being done *by* or *for* the press is extraordinary. No one wants to be the last on the block to have his own poll, even if its findings are no more rewarding or revealing than a half-dozen others already available. Thus we have ABC and Lou Harris, AP and NBC, *Time* magazine and Yankelovich, CBS and the *New York Times,* the *Washington Post's* very own poll, and ditto the *Los Angeles Times.*

This would be harmless enough if it were not for one terrible truth: Once a newspaper (or broadcast station) has a polling capacity, it feels obliged to use it, often to duplicate the work of others or to do research that isn't worth doing.

Thus, for example, my own newspaper carried a front-page story recently reporting that Carter had hit his all-time low in the *Time* magazine poll. (We are owned by *Time* magazine.) He had already reached that unhappy state in the Gallup and Harris polls, and now the "news" was that the results had been duplicated by still another national poll.

POLLING ON THE ISSUES

Not to slight our competitors here at the *Post,* I noticed the other day a report on a survey telling us that X number of congressmen believe the energy crisis is real. I never doubted that, and my eyes glazed over, as did those, I suspect, of many readers.

One particular problem with the proliferation of polls at the disposal of editors is that editors are such suckers for figures in neat columns: Give them the most obvious stuff and they will rush it into print so long as there is a nifty table to go along with it. That is a lesson every young reporter learns when he writes about how many miles of sewer laterals have been laid in the suburbs in the last five years.

In 1976 there were two classic cases of what I like to call "technical exclusives"—meaning stories nobody else would bother to have that came out of polls. One was carried under the headline: "Over Half in Poll Feel Distrustful of Government." Everyone already knew that the voters don't trust their politicians, and now we had front-page evidence of just how many felt that way. All that was lacking to comfort the most literal-minded editor was some evidence as to just how many voters *ought to* distrust their government. The second classic ran under this headline: "Poll Finds Voters Judging '76 Rivals on Personality." Imagine that. Any reporter or politician or political consultant in the country could have told us that, but the poll performed the questionable service of putting numbers to the phenomenon.

My point here is not to argue against the press looking into (1) the extent of alienation in the electorate, or (2) the criteria voters were using to make their decisions. Both of these are legitimate stories, but how much better they would have been had they been reported with specificity and color buttressed by the research.

Those are not isolated examples. There was a national poll a few weeks ago, for example, that reported that a plurality of the voters believed that President Carter's Cabinet shakeup would make no substantial difference in the way the administration operated. What the people were telling us was, hell, *we* can't tell. And, of course, they couldn't. Knowing the precise number who felt that way—it was 42 percent—tells us nothing.

I would agree that these are examples of harmless exercises, if you can classify boring your readers as harmless. In other cases, however, newspapers use opinion surveys so uncritically that they mislead their readers. Again, I would say that when I make that complaint about us, I make it even more heavily about television.

The most glaring examples are those in which we set up straw men. My favorite from 1976 were those polls that told us that if Hubert Humphrey had been a candidate in, for example, the Pennsylvania primary, he would have won it. That is patent nonsense, and no one knew it better than Hubert Humphrey; it was one of the reasons he didn't run. What he recognized, and what anyone in politics knows, is that a candidate in the abstract is one thing, a candidate out on the streets—warts and all—is quite another.

To some extent, the same complaint can be made about the presidential preference polls that are a staple of the early stages of a campaign. We have been told *ad nauseum,* for example, that Gerald Ford is one of the top two Republicans, just ahead of or just behind Ronald Reagan.

I don't question the data, which I am sure are accurate. But what everyone in this room (but not all of our readers) knows is that these polls reflect the public's familiarity with the names far more than any considered decision about their ultimate choice for the 1980 presidential nomination. Now it is also true that many—although by no means all—news reports on such polls, as well as the polls themselves, make that point about name recognition. But that is fine print when the burden of the story is projecting a false impression of the situation in the Republican Party.

What this line of argument leads to is a somewhat more general complaint about newspaper and, even more particularly, television use of survey research: the consistent failure of the media to provide a detailed and understandable qualification of the meaning of the data.

The polls tend to give a far more clearcut picture of a situation than is usually justified. In the polling business, I understand, it is naughty to have too many undecided so there are varying degrees of pressure applied on respondents to make a choice or have an opinion. I recognize that there are valid measures of intensity that can be used to qualify these choices or opinions, but my point is that these nuances are lost in newspaper translation. We learn that 32 percent of Americans are against fluoride in their water, not that only 2 per cent really give a damn.

We often fail to provide a proper context for understanding polls. One of the things that both pollsters and newspaper reporters quickly discover is that most people don't know a great deal about what is going on—and that their opinions might be quite different if they did. Even intensive coverage by the news media doesn't change that, particularly if the subject matter is complex and the terminology foreign to the layman.

Another classic case emerged from a survey done last winter immediately after President Carter's budget had been submitted to Congress. The newspapers had been crammed full of articles and columns about Carter's turn toward defense spending and away from social spending, but the survey data showed that most people thought the opposite—that he favored more social programs and lower defense spending—and that was duly reported. What was interesting about this was not the figures but what they might suggest—that is, (1) that Carter was not communicating successfully, (2) that Carter was so artful in communicating that he convinced the public black was white, or (3) that the press did a poor job in reporting on his budget. Any of those theories would have made a better story than what we reported.

Journalism or Social Science?

The lack of knowledge about or interest in current affairs means that we are, on many issues, implying a much more informed decision by the public than has been made. For example, we publish polls regularly about the views of the citizenry on the Strategic Arms Limitation Treaty. What I know from personal experience, however, and what every pollster discovers quickly enough, is that most people don't have the foggiest idea what is in SALT II or what equities are involved in the ratification decision. It is true that the polls point out that many voters say they don't know enough about the issue to have an opinion, but what we convey is nonetheless a picture of an electorate wrestling with some great decision, coming down this way one month and that way the next.

Still another problem with newspaper use of data is that the polls are rarely interpreted with the kind of sophistication that a pollster would employ in explaining his research to a client candidate.

At the most elementary level, this is obvious in those [recent] polls that show Jimmy Carter now 4 points ahead of Ronald Reagan—the reverse of the findings a month or so ago. We know, but do not say, that this "lead" is so tenuous and artificial that it probably will vanish next week when Ronald Reagan declares his candidacy and gets his inning on the Walter Cronkite show. We also know that a 4-point "lead"—given the margin for error in that size sample—is probably meaningless. But we don't want to say, as pollsters or newspapers, that Carter vs. Reagan would be anyone's guess right now. We insist instead on choosing a winner, at least for the moment. (It is stunning to find out how seriously the White House took that finding. All of a sudden their whole view of their situation in the contest for the Democratic nomination was altered by the fact that Carter was four points ahead of Reagan rather than four points behind him. God help us all!)

Nor do we follow the data to the back of the book, or

computer printout. An example: A poll shows only a small minority of the people say they are concerned about Chappaquiddick and what it suggests about how Kennedy might conduct himself as president. The stories on that poll all say the same thing: no problem. In fact, however, if you pull the threads out to the end, you may find that perhaps 4 or 5 percent of the voters who ordinarily could be expected to support Kennedy are defecting because of the Chappaquiddick or some related issue. Although we know that in the ordinary presidential election a defection of even two or three points can be fatal to a candidate, that makes for a complex, tedious story, so we choose to go with the big picture and mislead our readers.

The pollsters say, of course, that this is not their fault, that the data are all there if we want to root them out and explain them. But that is only partially true. It is both our faults: that of the press if we publish information without proper analysis, and that of the pollster who panders to our weakness for neat columns of figures that make sense out of the world of politics.

Again, I am not arguing that the pollster should not make all the surveys his heart desires and his clients will finance. Nor am I saying that the pollster has a responsibility to see that the press does a more mature job of handling the material. What I am saying is that many of those in the opinion research business are too happy to oblige, even encourage, the worst instincts of the press to oversimplify by giving a stamp of respectability to figures they don't take very seriously themselves.

I would like to see polls used intelligently by the press although there are times when I think that what newspapers should do is publish somewhere back in the paper an agate-type box similar to those used to list the ten leading hitters in each league during the baseball season. It would record the latest from Gallup and Roper and Harris and Field, the *Post* and the *Times,* each network, with all the caveats about sample size, methods, probabilities, and the wording of the questions. When someone started hitting .400, we would assign a reporter to do a story about it, just as a baseball writer would cover Rod Carew. If someone had a terrible slump, we would make a point of writing about that, too. Otherwise, the figures would just be there for the editors who like neat tables and the political junkies.

That, of course, isn't practical, so the next best thing is what the *Post* has done, and we are doing: assign someone not necessarily to do our own polls, but to follow polls closely and write about them intelligently, if only occasionally.

Most of all, however, I would be eternally vigilant if I were running my newspaper (which I am not) about allowing the data to be used as a substitute for thorough reporting or for the judgment of an experienced reporter with the proper sense of detachment.

There are simply some things that cannot be quantified. I remember particularly a poll in 1976 that reported that candidate Jimmy Carter had not suffered any political loss from the "lust in my heart" interview in *Playboy* magazine. I don't doubt that is what the research showed. Nor would I argue that a large number of voters turned away from Carter because of that episode. But what everyone in the political community knew was that the incident changed the way people looked at Jimmy Carter. It was a first-class political story, which is something we rarely can get from a column of figures.

Irving Crespi

The Case
of Presidential Popularity

EDITORIAL judgments about newsworthiness are central to the existence of presidential popularity ratings, the wide publicity given to them, and their significance for public policy. Over the years, these judgments have favored hard, spot news—especially about controversial competitive events—and "human interest" stories about personalities. Polls that seem to provide advance clues to who is going to win the next election meet this double criterion of newsworthiness. This explains why the horserace aspect of election campaigns has long dominated the reporting of poll results, most importantly presidential popularity ratings.

We must also take account of the fact that public opinion polling was started by the news media and has always depended upon them as the primary source of financial support. The first documented poll in the United States was conducted in 1824 by the *Harrisburg Pennsylvanian* to measure voting preferences in that year's presidential election. Today, most public opinion polls are conducted under contract to the news media or are conducted directly by them. This financial dependence of polls upon the news media explains the influence upon polling of the proverbial guy with the green eyeshade, to whom "if it isn't happening, it isn't news." His acceptance is crucial to the publication of polls, so pollsters have always had to be sensitive to what *he* thought was good enough to print. The resultant *ad hoc* day-by-day interaction between editor and pollster has been the focal influence on the way public opinion polling is conducted today. If we are to understand the role of presidential popularity ratings, we must also turn our attention to how they emerged out of the informal interaction between editor and pollster.

The Origin of Presidential Popularity Ratings

The fact that American national politics runs on a four-year cycle geared to presidential elections led to the invention of presidential popularity ratings by the Gallup Poll. This cycle creates a business problem for public opinion polls: What can they sell to their news media clients during the three off-years? From the beginning of modern polling in 1935 right up to the present, news editors have displayed little interest in most non-political polls. Thus, newspaper subscriptions to the Gallup Poll typically fell off sharply during the interim years, and the few remaining subscribers often did not publish non-political poll reports. This created considerable pressure to find newsworthy topics to poll on during non-election years. (Even today polls on candidate standings, including those with little or no methodological merit, as well as leaked privately commissioned polls, are consistently considered good copy.) While polls on issues and impending legislation are obvious possibilities, editorial interest in them was relatively limited, perhaps because editors do not believe such polls provide any inkling of whether a bill will be passed. Human interest topics—such as fashion, "the war between the sexes," health, most admired man and woman, and leisure—became standard fall-backs for the Gallup Poll. But its greatest success was achieved by inventing election-oriented questions about candidates that could be asked during the years between presidential elections.

Some of the variety of "off-year election" questions experimented with by the Gallup Poll during the 1930s and the 1940s have become integral to the political scene. These include "trial heats," which test the early voting strength of prospective candidates in direct opposition to each other; "primary tests," which present lists of potential candidates to identify the leading choices for nomination among rank-and-file Democrats and Republicans; and popularity or approval ratings of incumbents. One characteristic that these questions have in common is their focus on political personalities rather than on issues. When the first presidential approval questions were asked, the expectation was that they would meet the "natural human interest in ... people in the news—especially the President."[1] The development of off-year approval ratings into the standardized form now used by the Gallup Poll was halting and unplanned. The Gallup Poll first asked presidential approval questions in July 1939, a year before the 1940 nominating convention, when it asked "In general, do you approve or disapprove of Franklin Roosevelt as president?"[2] This question was asked four more times at irregular intervals in the period immediately before and after the 1940 presidential election—in December 1939, January 1940, January 1941 and April 1941. A different version ("In general, do you approve or disapprove the way Franklin Roosevelt is handling his job as president today?") was also asked following Roosevelt's reelection—in February, June, and August 1941. No further "approval" ratings were obtained for Roosevelt during his final four years of office.

Harry S Truman's first approval rating was taken in June 1945, about two months after he assumed office, but a second measurement was not taken until March 1947, about 16 months before that 1948 nominating convention.[3] After that, approval of Truman was measured more frequently but still not on a regular sechdule. The intermittent nature of these early measurements reflects their tentative, unplanned development. In 1950, only three measurements were taken. By 1951, however, enough interest had been generated in these ratings that seven measures of public approval of Truman were taken in that year, though on an irregular schedule. Thus, about twelve years elapsed from the first approval rating taken regarding Roosevelt to when these ratings became a regular, though intermittent, feature of the Gallup Poll.

Journalism or Social Science?

During most of Dwight D. Eisenhower's years in office, approval ratings were taken on the average about every two months. Their frequency slowly increased, so that nine measurements were taken in 1951. However, it became the practice *not* to take approval ratings during election campaigns because of conflict with trial heat reports: Eisenhower's approval ratings were consistently higher than his standing in trial heats, an apparent discrepancy which editors found difficult to reconcile. Rather than attempt to explain the difference between the two measurements, approval ratings were dropped during campaigns in favor of the more newsworthy trial heats.

Eisenhower's consistently high approval ratings raised the question of how he compared with previous presidents. I had joined the Gallup Poll in 1956, and one of my early assignments was to compile all the prior ratings for Eisenhower, as well as for Roosevelt and Truman. This not only served the immediate journalistic purpose of creating an interesting news story about prominent political personalities, it also established a trend line for reporting future measurements. In this way, journalistic interest in presidential approval ratings was furthered by two reporting techniques, namely, highlighting the trend in the incumbent's standing and comparing his record with that of previous presidents.

The result of these reporting techniques was that the ratings were perceived as measures of comparative political strength and, inferentially, electability. The monthly ratings became a sort of continuing surrogate election, even in the absence of any avowed opponent, as a presumptive "fever chart" of the incumbent's political strength. Journalistic demand was thereby created for election polls even when there is no election by the invention of a technique that makes polling a "continuing election."[4] The journalistic success of Gallup's monthly approval ratings is evident in their adoption by other polls. Today, the Harris, Roper,

NBC/Associated Press, CBS/New York Times, and myriad other public opinion polls each produces its own presidential approval rating. With the exception of trial heats, these ratings are at this time undoubtedly the most prominent of all poll results, often receiving front-page treatment and avidly followed by the incumbent presidents as well as other politicians.[5]

Most polls have borrowed from Gallup the concept of rating how the public thinks the incumbent is "handling his job as president." (Chart 1) The CBS/New York Times Poll has adopted Gallup's question outright. The Harris Survey developed its own version by using a four-point rating scale to measure approval of the job the incumbent is doing as president. The NBC/Associated Press question is clearly modeled on the Harris version, while the Washington Post uses a five-point "report card" scale. (It is noteworthy that, in response to emerging journalistic interest in rating scales, Gallup occasionally asks a follow-up question to measure intensity of approval or disapproval, thus converting its dichotomy into a four-point scale.)[6] Roper has taken a different approach from Gallup's, one intended to be more directly related to ultimate voting behavior, by using a four-point scale to measure the extent to which one rates himself a supporter or a critic of the incumbent. With each poll charting its own trend line of the president's public standing, there now exist a number of simultaneous, sometimes conflicting, "continuing elections" competing with each other for public attention.

In recent years, interest has also developed in more sophisticated applications of the approval rating concept. In addition to overall appraisal, ratings are obtained for separate facets of presidential responsibility such as foreign affairs, the economy, and energy. Because Congress's performance is now also being rated, it is possible to compare the relative public standing of the executive and legislative branches. Despite these developments, however, journalistic interest continues to focus on whether the president's

CHART I

Question Wordings Used By Six Polls to Measure Presidential Popularity

Gallup
"Do you approve or disapprove of the way (*Carter*) is handling his job as President?" ("Is that approve/disapprove strongly, or approve/disapprove somewhat?")

Harris
"How would you rate the job (*Carter*) is doing as President? Would you say he is doing an excellent, pretty good, or only fair, or a poor job?"

Washington Post
"Suppose you were to grade President (*Carter*) A, B, C, D or F for the way he is handling his job as President. What grade would you give him?"

NBC/Associated Press
"What kind of job do you think (*Jimmy Carter*) is doing as President... do you think he is doing an excellent job, a good job, only a fair job, or do you think he is doing a poor job?"

CBS/New York Times
"Do you approve or disapprove of the way (*Jimmy Carter*) is handling his job as President?"

Roper
"How do you feel about President (*Carter*)? At the present time would you describe yourself as a strong Carter supporter, a moderate Carter supporter, a moderate critic of Carter, or a strong critic of Carter?"

standing in "the popularity polls" is improving or declining. The continuing election remains at the center of poll reporting.

Inconsistent and Contradictory Approval Ratings

With the proliferation of polls, each with its own method for measuring the incumbent president's public standing, journalists (and politicians) have been faced with problems in interpreting the sometimes inconsistent and contradictory reports. These reports differ in two ways. First there are *absolute* differences in the proportion that approves the president's performance in office. Second, there are *relative* differences in the direction and magnitude of change, regardless of what the absolute difference may be. In either case, assessing a president's voting strength on the basis of approval ratings is complicated when each of half a dozen polls issues a report that differs in some way from all the others.

The journalist and the politician want to know the size of the "real" proportion that approves the incumbent's performance, and which poll does the best job of measuring that proportion, just as they want to know which is the most accurate pre-election poll. However, the fact is that there is no one "real" proportion that approves a president's performance in office. Unlike voting preferences, which involve a choice between specified alternatives, judgments of performance in office fall along a continuum of approval-disapproval. The measured proportion with a favorable attitude can vary appreciably, depending on how that continuum is divided.

Barry Sussman and Gary Orren have reported an interesting experiment which provides evidence that the kind of rating scale used significantly affects presidential approval scores.[7] In this experiment, the proportion of favorable ratings, the ratio of favorable to unfavorable ratings, and the proportion of "don't know" all varied according to whether Gallup's dichotomy, Harris's four-point scale, or the Post's five-point scale was used. The Gallup method produced a favorable rating of 62 percent for Carter, appreciably higher than either Harris's 48 percent or the Post's 41 percent. On the other hand, the Harris method produced a 4 percent "don't know" compared with 10 percent for Gallup and 8 percent for the Post. (While Sussman and Orren did not use Gallup's probe which converts the dichotomy into a four-point scale, it is obvious that if they had the results would have been different from those produced by using Harris's four-point scale.)

What is not clear from these data is how these differences relate to Carter's political strength. Unfortunately, there is no direct evidence available that would answer the question: How does the approval-disapproval continuum correlate with voting behavior? What evidence does exist suggests that there is no straightforward relation. In a December, 1978, Gallup Poll, 51 percent said they approved of the way Carter was handling his job as president. In the *same* poll, Carter beat Ford in a "trial heat" 52%-39%, and Reagan 57%-35%.[8] On the face of it, this would suggest that the Gallup question might be slightly *under*estimating Carter's voting strength among the general electorate. However, as mentioned earlier a very different pattern existed during Eisenhower's incumbency. For example, in March, 1965, Gallup reported Eisenhower beating Kefauver in a "trial heat" 55%-39%, and Stevenson 61%-37%, while an April, 1956, poll gave Eisenhower a 71 percent approval rating.[9] These 1956 data would indicate that Gallup's approval question *over*estimates voting appeal.

What may be the case is that an unpopular president gets votes from loyalists within his own party who do not approve his performance. Conversely, a popular president may lose votes to loyalists of the opposing party even though they voice approval. Also, trial heat results in both 1956 and 1978 differed significantly depending on the identity of the opponent. Finally, account must be taken of the fact that the approval ratings are based on samples of all adults of voting age, while the trial heats are based on registered voters only. In an election, of course, it is only the opinions of those who vote that count, not the total electorate. In all probability it is the combined effects of these factors—party loyalty, the competitive strength of a specific opponent, and turnout—that helps explain why, to use a state election as an example, Brendan Byrne was able to achieve a substantial margin of victory when he was re-elected Governor of New Jersey in 1977, despite his abysmally low approval rating in the New Jersey Poll.[10] The only safe conclusion to be drawn at this time is that approval ratings are imperfect measures of voting strength. The obvious questions for us to ask then are: What do approval ratings measure and why should attention be paid to them?

Before turning to these questions, however, we should take note of some other reasons why approval ratings may differ, reasons that are often overlooked. One important influence on survey results is the position of a question in the questionnaire. For example, the identical question, asked of matched samples, can be expected to get different proportions approving Carter's performance depending on whether it is preceded by questions about the Camp David agreement or inflation. To avoid such biasing influences, the best procedure is to have the presidential approval question lead off the interview, a practice that is in fact followed by many polls. Information about question position is not normally reported, however, so at present it is impossible to assess the extent to which conflicting approval ratings have been caused by differences in position.

The fact that some polls (such as Gallup, Harris, and Roper) are conducted in person, while others (such as CBS/New York Times, NBC/Associated Press and The Washington Post) are conducted by telephone, must also be considered. The fact is that non-telephone households are disproportionately poor, black, and rural.[11] It was also my experience while at Gallup that, compared with our personal interview surveys, our telephone surveys tended to overrepresent the college-educated and underrepresent those who had not gone beyond grade school. Undoubtedly as a result of these socio-economic differences, our telephone surveys also tended to be more Republican. To control for this source of bias, we used standard statistical controls, namely, "weighting" the obtained sample.

Another difference between personal interview and telephone surveys is that the latter are typically characterized by higher refusal rates. It is *considerably less expensive* to call back "not at homes" in telephone surveys, however, so some telephone polls attempt repeated call-backs when conducting their surveys. An additional difference emerges because it is sometimes impossible for an interviewer to gain physical entry into middle-class high rise apartments, a problem that is not encountered in telephone surveys. It is therefore not surprising that, even though CBS/ New York Times and Gallup use the same question wording, their results are often different. The extent to which conflicting approval ratings result from differences in sample design and interviewing methods is a question that merits more attention than it has been given so far.

Survey professionals have long been aware of the way in which even minor variations in question wording can lead to significant measurement differences. That is to say, rather than being surprised at the fact that polling organizations which use different question wordings obtain conflicting measures of presidential approval, we should be surprised if there weren't any conflicts. Commenting on the problems of analysis that occur when different question wordings are used to measure the same thing, James Davis observed that these problems reflect our lack of skill in dealing with the precise sensitivity of people to the specific wording of questions asked of them.[12] Rather than being an indicator of an inherent weakness in the survey method, measurement differences resulting from variations in question wording demonstrate the precision of the method. The challenge is to determine how people *understand* the question asked of them and how these understandings may differ from what we *thought* we were asking. In this spirit, let us compare those questions that adopt the Gallup model by asking about how the president is "handling his job" with Roper's question as to whether one is a supporter or critic of the president. Such a comparison will enable us to understand better just what is really being measured by approval ratings.

One basic difference between the Gallup and Roper questions is that the former asks one to rate *the president* whereas the latter asks for a rating of *oneself* in relation to the president. The Gallup model asks for an assessment of the president's performance, but unlike Roper's question does not ask for a statement of political allegiance. Any conclusions we draw from Gallup's question about political allegiance are inferences based on assumptions we make as to how people decide their allegiances. In contrast, the Roper model relates more directly to where one's allegiance lies, but does not explicitly ask about the source of that allegiance. It seems reasonable, in both cases, to assume that there should be a correlation between how one rates Carter's performance and whether one is a political adherent of his. It is necessary to remind ourselves, however, that political support derives from a number of factors, not only from how one evaluates performance in office.[13] In any event, it is clear that the Gallup and Roper approaches seek to measure a president's public standing from different perspectives, so that while we would expect them to produce generally similar results, we would also expect statistically significant differences between them.

Mention should also be made of the effect of a poll's timing on approval ratings. Although this has received considerable attention in the press, there is one aspect of the role of timing that warrants emphasis. Public opinion can change sharply in reaction to important events, so approval ratings taken just before and just after an event sometimes differ sharply. It is therefore important to differentiate polls taken on the heels of an event from those conducted after even a short lapse of time. When making such differentiations, we need to note that some polling organizations are relatively unlikely to conduct "same day" polls. These organizations conduct their surveys on a regular schedule so that, except by chance, they do not ordinarily measure the immediate effects of events on presidential approval ratings. In contrast, other polling organizations, such as network telephone polls, are in a better position to go into the field on very short notice, and occasionally do so for reasons of journalistic rivalry. Over a period of time, differences in scheduling could lead to a systematic difference in approval ratings among the various polling organizations.

The significance of this becomes apparent when we remember that political media events are often staged with the express hope that they will improve a president's approval rating, as in fact they typically do. Such improvements, however, are often ephemeral: a poll taken immediately after such an event may be significantly more favorable than one taken a few days later. For example, the trend line in Lyndon Johnson's approval ratings followed a sawtooth pattern, with short bursts of increased approval in response to particular events periodically interrupting a long-term slide. Two organizations with different interviewing schedules could easily have shown very different short-term trends in Johnson's standing.

In light of all the differences in methods used by public opinion polls to measure presidential approval, the similarities in their results are more impressive than their conflicts. In general, they mostly agree on the general trend of public appraisal, despite specific differences. Yet public attention has focused more on the differences than on the similarities. In a sense this is normal, since measurement differences are always confusing. However, the intensity of criticism in Washington and among the news media when polls report different approval ratings suggests that something more than normal response is involved. It is likely that the use of approval ratings as a continuing election, testing the continuing validity of the mandate for office conferred by the last election, is what explains the intensity of public criticism. Those whose careers and decisions are dependent on the electorate's mandate inevitably want to know what that mandate *really* is and are understandably disturbed by conflicting reports all of which purport to be objective and scientific.

The Meaning of Presidential Approval Ratings

The leadership structure of a functioning democracy encompasses two functions: a head of state and a head of government. In democracies such as Great Britain, France, or Italy there is a prime minister who serves as head of government and a president or constitutional monarch who serves as titular head of state. The American presidency is unique in that the two functions are combined in one office. Perforce, assessments of a president's performance in office encompass judgments about how the state, as well as the government, is functioning. It is not necessary for the public to understand this dual function for it to respond to the resultant political realities. Approval or disapproval of a president therefore relates to more than whether one supports his administration's policies and programs. Approval also relates to one's general satisfaction with the state of the nation. Thus, during the decade 1953-1962, in which the nation was at peace, employment high, and inflation limited, Eisenhower and Kennedy both received high approval ratings, higher than their voting strength as measured in trial heats. Moreover, at times when the president's role as head of state predominates, such as during the Cuban missile crisis, a "rally round the flag" reaction leads typically to an improvement in the president's approval rating. Conversely, dissatisfaction with the state of the nation, as during the internal disorders of the last years of Johnson's administration or the current runaway inflation, leads to depressed approval ratings.

The voting strength of an incumbent president, it goes without saying, depends to a considerable degree upon the state of the nation. As *elected* head of state, the president cannot avoid responsibility for its condition whether or not caused by his administration's policies and actions. Nonetheless, clarity requires distinguishing between an incumbent's voting strength *per se* and what can be called the "political climate." The latter refers to whether public opinion is characterized by optimism and confidence, conflict and dissension, or confused pessimism—that is, it refers to the nation's political cohesiveness and strength.

Just as the presidency has two functions, presidential approval ratings have two comparable dimensions, with any particular rating identifying the intersection of the two. Thus presidential approval ratings, although they are commonly treated by the news media almost exclusively as measures of voting strength, are to a considerable degree also a measure of the political climate. Gallup's early experiments with alternative question wordings were specifically concerned with this fact. His first version, "In general, do you approve or disapprove of Roosevelt as president?" was dropped since many people expressed approval of Roosevelt not because they supported him but because he was the elected president.[14] The question finally adopted, which focuses on how the *job* of president is being handled, is only a partial solution.

In any event, emphasis by the news media on the head-of-government dimension of approval ratings to the exclusion of the head-of-state dimension intensifies the normal concern of any administration about its voting strength. Such an intensification can lead, and has led, to a consuming preoccupation with partisan politics. To the extent that political attention focuses narrowly on the latest approval rating as an indicator of the president's voting strength, there is a strong danger that the incumbent's normal efforts to shore up any apparent voting weaknesses will take precedence over concern about the state of the nation. Such an ordering of priorities can be self-defeating, since satisfaction with the president's performance as head of state is an important component of his approval rating (and, ultimately, of his voting strength). Nonetheless, political realities create strong pressures for such a reordering.

Presidential approval ratings have created a pseudo-parlimentary situation, whereby the president faces a monthly vote of confidence from the total electorate. While not binding in any sense, this vote of confidence is accepted by both politicians and political analysts as an indicator of the president's political clout and, therefore, of his ability to govern effectively. For example, any change in his rating is likely to be reflected in a president's ability to push his legislative programs through Congress. It is not surprising that, under these circumstances, incumbent administrations come to feel that they have no choice but to behave as if they are *always* in the midst of an election campaign.

Unlike conventional news reports that inform the public what has happened, presidential approval ratings create news that would not otherwise exist, and in a way that affects the balance of political power in Washington. What is anomalous about this development is that it has been created by journalists' use of poll reports. The pressure on the president to keep his ratings high, and to judge how successfully he is governing on how well he is doing in the polls, has in effect been created by editors in whose judgment the most newsworthy aspects of public opinion polls is their ability to chart the horserace aspect of politics. But, as we have seen, approval ratings are an imperfect measure of a president's voting strength, while preoccupation with elections has diverted attention from the totality of what approval ratings do measure.

In addition to their partisan significance, approval ratings are also in part an indicator not merely of presidential voting strength but also of the political state of the nation. When Nixon's approval rating plummeted during the final weeks of his administration, this was more than a measure of personal political weakness. It also was an indicator of a constitutional crisis, one that was resolved only by his resignation. Similarly, the high approval ratings characteristic of a new administration's early months are as much a vote of confidence in the legitimacy of the electoral process as they are a sign of agreement with that administration's proposed policies. Viewed in this perspective, approval ratings can be a very useful tool for political analysts.

Conclusion

So long as the newsworthiness of presidential approval ratings depends on their dealings with the horse race aspect of elections, we can expect that they will continue to needlessly divert the attention of office holders from the substance of governing to the political struggle for power. The struggle for power, of course, is intrinsic to politics, but in a democracy we expect it to be a means to effective government and not an all-encompassing end in itself. Public opinion polls, including those that measure presidential approval, can be used to do much more than chart political horse races. Their most constructive role is to provide guidance to those in office, and those seeking office, concerning the public's aspirations, concerns, priorities, unsatisfied wants and needs—that is, to further the democratic setting of policy goals. Public opinion polls can also be used to clarify the reasons underlying public preferences among alternative means of implementing policy and so contribute to the development of acceptable government programs. Using polls in this way would strengthen democratic government, rather than undermine it.

Even now the existence of presidential approval ratings has made government more responsive to the electorate than would otherwise have been the case. Presidents have felt a continuing pressure to concern themselves with public opinion precisely because approval ratings are reported monthly. What has gone wrong is that the substantive reasons underlying shifts in public approval have been virtually ignored while journalistic attention has been riveted on the political horserace. It would be unfortunate if, in reaction to this misfocusing of attention, approval ratings were discontinued. Instead, what is needed are polls that go beyond the mere measurement of the public's evaluation of a president to the analysis of the substance of public concerns. The challenge to the journalistic profession is to find ways to make such a use of polls interesting to its audience—that is, to make it newsworthy.

Notes

1. Conversation with Dr. George Gallup, September 23, 1979.
2. George Gallup, *Gallup Opinion Index* NY: Random House, 1972 Vol. 1, p. 166 and Index Vol. 3, p. 2378.
3. *Ibid*, Vol. 1, p. 512 and *Index* Vol. 3, p. 2384.
4. See Harold Mendelsohn and Irving Crespi, *Polls, Television and the New Politics,* Chandler Publishing Company 1970, pp. 43-49 for a discussion of polls as continuing elections.
5. In the past, the White House would telephone to try to get advance reports, but that practice has been discontinued.
6. An interesting footnote is that during the 1950s Gallup had experimentally used the Stapel Scale—a ten-point numerical scale that measures direction and intensity of attitude simultaneoulsy—to measure presidential popularity. Even though he considers this technique far superior to the question currently used, he

has used it infrequently because of the difficulty of explaining it in news reports. (Conversation with Dr. George Gallup, September 23, 1979.)

7. Barry Sussman, "Distortion in Popularity Polls," The *Washington Post,* February 12, 1978, Gary R. Orren, "Presidential Popularity Ratings: Another View," *Public Opinion,* May/June 1978, Vol. 1, No. 22, p. 35.

8. *Gallup Political Index,* January 1979.

9. *The Gallup Poll 1935-1972,* Vol. 2, p. 1414-1415, 1422. As it turned out, Eisenhower ultimately defeated Stevenson by 58%-42% margin.

10. Byrne received 57 percent of votes cast, despite the fact that in April, 1977, only 17 percent had given him a positive rating in answer to the question, "Overall, how good a job do you think the governor of New Jersey—Brendan Byrne—is doing—excellent, good, only fair, or poor?" Stephen A. Salmore, "The Contest for Governor: Why Bateman Lost," *New Jersey Magazine* November/December 1977, Vol. 7, No. 3 & 4, p. 4.

11. Marie L. Monsees and James T. Massey, "Application of Personal Interview Definitions to a Telephone Survey," *Design and Collection Issues in NCHS Surveys: A Session to Honor the Memory of Elijah White,* Department of Health, Education and Welfare, Public Health Service; Office of Health Research, Statistics, and Technology; National Center for Health Statistics (undated).

12. Remarks at National Council on Public Polls Seminar, "Polls About Politics," May, 1976.

13. Three separate factors in voting decisions are party identification, issues, and attitude toward the candidates. See: Angus Campbell, Gerald Gurin, and Warren E. Miller, *The Voter Decides,* (Evanston: Row, Peterson and Company, 1954).

14. Personal conversation with Dr. George Gallup. September 23, 1979. A second problem with the first version was that others answered the questions by saying that they liked, or disliked, Roosevelt—as distinct from whether they approved or disapproved. (Personal conversation with Paul Perry, October 24, 1979.)

Comments
and Observations

ITHIEL DE SOLA POOL: It's always easier for a commentator if he can be a critic and disagree with some of the things that were said in the papers. I'm afraid I don't have that advantage. I found them all penetrating and to the point. The emphasis in all three papers was on the inclination to oversimplify poll results and to focus on the horse-race aspect of politics; the remedies proposed by all include more analysis and more substantive information. What struck me is that in making this case no attention was paid to a third party in addition to the pollers and the press, namely, the academic researchers.

There is a triad of three kinds of professionals, all of them involved in some way trying to explicate the process of public opinion—the pollers, the journalists, and the scholars. To a large extent they are all trying to answer the same questions and all are using each other. We scholars are certainly enormously dependent on both files of newspapers and files of public opinion polls such as those in The Roper Center. But the reverse is also true. I don't think anybody who is doing political public opinion analysis today can help but be very dependent on a large mass of important research done on voting and election behavior by Lazarsfeld and Berelson,* on the one hand, and by the Center for Political Studies at the University of Michigan, on the other. This scholarly work uses standard survey techniques but analyzes them in much greater depth and much more slowly than the press is able to do. This activity has contributed to

---

* Paul F. Lazarsfeld, Bernard Berelson and Hazel Gaudet, *The People's Choice* (New York: Duell, Sloan and Pearce, 1944); Bernard R. Berelson, Paul F. Lazarsfeld and William N. McPhee, *Voting* (Chicago: University of Chicago Press, 1954).

the backlog of understanding in terms of which current work is done. So we do have a triad, all members of which share certain common problems and depend on one another.

I was rather pleased that while problems were pointed to in the presentations nobody was proposing any flat rules for solving the problems. I don't think there are flat rules. There are problems and there are trade-offs. Among his concerns Bud Roper mentioned the conflict of interest and the bias that are introduced by the fact of newspapers owning their own polls and doing their own polling. That is a very real problem which entails very real trade-offs. Newspaper ownership of polls enables the papers to incorporate the process of understanding through polling right into their normal organizational structure and partly explains the growth in poll acceptance by the press that Bud was referring to. The severe disadvantages of this situation need not be discussed in a hypothetical way; we can look at things that have happened in countries where newspaper owner-ship of polls is normal. In Japan and Great Britain most polling has been done by the media themselves from the beginning and the problems that have emerged are exactly those that Bud is concerned about. That is, each paper tends to see the world in terms of its own poll and reports as if its poll were the truth, disregarding the others. The failure of a poll in such situations can have a severe effect upon the medium itself. That has occurred in this country with the *Literary Digest* poll.

There is also the problem of what professional standards should be applied at the interface of polling and journalism. I can't argue that no journalist should ever do the kind of semi-polling that journalists do when they walk up and down the street and interview 20 people in different houses. This is a useful and good way of getting information, and it probably improves the resulting story. And journalists' understanding of more scientific polling can only help. It is crucial, however, that journalists' self-awareness of the problems in such pseudo-sampling be increased.

I am worried about rules that we make for ourselves being artifically restrictive, but let me note that there is also the possibility of rules being imposed on us. At the moment, those of us who are doing social science research in academic settings are threatened by an extraordinary set of regulations that the Department of Health, Education and Welfare is proposing which would require that we be subject to prior review—that is, the Department would impose prior restraint—on all interview research except polls using formal instruments.

All these problems lead back to the central question with which our three speakers were concerned: the possible misinterpretation, oversimplification, and lack of in-depth analysis in newspaper reporting of public opinion poll results. Polling is not the only field in which this is a problem. We can talk about the journalistic treatment of any technical subject, X. No matter what X may be, it is likely to be poorly reported and treated in inadequate depth. So pollers are not unique in this respect.

I was particularly intrigued by Irving Crespi's discussion of the polls as providing new social indicators. He used the words "pseudo-parliamentary situation." That's quite right: The use of polls as an indicator of how the president is doing, I would argue, has become a part of America's unwritten Constitution in exactly the same way that political parties have. Parties have been with us long enough so that few people doubt that parties are a part of our Constitution, and a great many people would be surprised to learn that they are not mentioned in the written Constitution. The poll question that puts the president under a fever barometer at all times has, perhaps, not been with us long enough to be fully constitutionalized but it is getting there. It is becoming a major factor in the structure of American government, and in the end I suspect it is likely to become an integral part of that structure.

This phenomenon too has its benefits and its disadvantages. The disadvantages Crespi pointed to very well when he indicated that it creates a continuous election. It politicizes the decision process in a way that wouldn't otherwise be the case. The advantages include democratizing the action of government, thereby making the executive branch more responsive to the way in which the public reacts to it.

We pay for that in governability. The president's short-run need to keep his barometer up will often inhibit him from taking those unpopular actions which long-run wisdom may require. In troubled times the president's rating will fall and his ability to mobilize the Congress and the nation be reduced at precisely the moment when leadership is most needed. These are some of the disadvantages; but we should not expect to be able to make simple univalent judgments of a development so important as a major Constitutional change. Whatever its advantages and disadvantages, the installation of a presidential performance thermometer has become a fact of American political life.

BARRY SUSSMAN: As Ithiel pointed out, all three of the speakers complained about the superficial way the news media report polls, and I agree that that is one of the great problems—the way we report polls. It is a problem not only for us but clearly for the pollsters themselves. I would like to make one point on that kind of criticism. Mr. Crespi said that part of the situation we have now was created by a financial dependence of pollsters on editors, which is a rather peculiar complaint. I am not sure I understand what happened, but I think that what came about as a result of that financial dependence was that the pollsters began doing these presidential popularity polls and other measures that they really knew were oversimplified and not proper measures. At least that's the implication I drew from what was said. We have the poor pollster, struggling like an artist to make a living, dependent on a newspaper editor who really doesn't know very much about polls to begin with and who is forcing the reporter to put out something that is misleading and over-simplified. I have a great problem with that part of your discussion. I don't think that editors generally force their own reporters to write articles that the reporters know are wrong or misleading; I've never seen an editor who does that. If there are any, they don't last too long.

I gather from all three of these discussions that the real difficulty lies in melding theory with practice. For example, Bud Roper told us that we are too quick on newspapers—we want something that is no more than four days old or we don't want to use it. Well, as it happens, we do use material more than four days old. But it was Bud Roper who I remember seeing on public TV immediately after a debate telling us what the public thought about who won. Now, there can't be anything more instant than a sample of 300 or 500 people in that kind of a situation.

Jack Germond, with whom I agree entirely on everything he mentioned, says that he relies heavily on polls. His complaint is about dull polls, or polls replacing political columnists, as I gather. I think the focus here is on the superficiality of polls as they are reported, and the complaint of that kind of bungling is frequently valid.

The discussion of presidential popularity polls highlights an increasingly important subject; we never know when we're going to be hit with one, as we found this week. I think most of you probably know a poll done by Yankelovich for *Time* magazine showed President Carter trailing Kennedy by 10 points among Democrats and Independents, and I imagine that just stopped in their tracks a lot of people who were thinking of moving from Carter to Kennedy, or had moved from Carter to Kennedy already. Of course a CBS poll came in the next day showing that there really had been no change at all among voters between Carter and Kennedy. I think that the public just doesn't know how to assess something like that.

Almost all the speakers focused on another key problem that we have with the reporting of polls: the notion that yours is the one that you must defend because it's yours, and it's the one you report to the exclusion of others. I don't think that happens all the time and I think that when it does happen, it is often the fault of the pollster rather than the news organization. For example: We have the Gallup Poll telling us that Gerald Ford is favored by one percentage point over Jimmy Carter. Well, the Gallup people know that that depends upon the nature of the turnout, but they just take their figures and make their best guess as to turnout. Somebody else will have different figures that again depend on turnout. Why must these organizations, all of which tell us they are not really in the business of predicting, make that kind of flat prediction? Why don't they just say, "We've got this range, and if everybody we interview comes out and votes, this is the way it looks; but if only a few people come out and vote, this is the way it is going to look." The need to rule out "don't knows," to have everybody with an opinion was mentioned. Well, in making those points, I think that there was a slight tendency among all three speakers to overgeneralize—to cluster all the news media together. Now, Jack Germond didn't do that—he said television is worse than newspapers! But the others certainly did. Bud, just as you would object to somebody saying "the polls say that the American people want SALT," I think it would be a little bit wrong to say, "The news media don't handle polls well." I think that some do, and some don't.

Floor
Discussion*

ROBERT J. CUNNINGHAM**: To what extent do you feel the approval polls may, in fact, generate the presidential horse race rather than document it? That is, to what extent do public opinion polls lead the process of opinion formation, especially in regard to the public's perception of the president?

IRVING CRESPI: This is the old bandwagon kind of issue, and there are two ways in which that question can be answered. If you are talking about the effect on the general public, I would maintain the general principle that the effect, if any, is trivial. On the other hand, particularly in a town like Washington, everyone is looking at polls, weighing them, and basing decisions on them. So sure, at the institutional level, the polls do have an effect.

JACK W. GERMOND: This is something people have been worried about for as long as I have been covering politics. The campaign finance law has changed things in this regard. It used to be that if a candidate continued to do poorly in the polls over a long period of time, his money would dry up. But now, because of public financing in presidential elections, any candidate can get enough money together with matching funds to make it through at least the first primary. A candidate has, therefore, one crack at a group of voters as opposed to respondents in the Gallup Poll. The result is that

---

* As mentioned in the Introduction, after each panel there were questions to the speakers and discussion from the floor. What follows here, and at the end of subsequent sections of the book, is an edited transcript of that give-and-take.

** Office of the Assistant Secretary for Policy, Department of Commerce.

people are not likely to be driven out of a race simply on the basis of poll standings. If that were the case, George Bush would have jumped out of a 30-story window already! Certainly John Anderson would have given up. Even Bob Dole is rolling the dice. They are all going to have enough to stay in through New Hampshire and see what happens. I don't think this effect of the polls is any longer a valid concern in presidential politics.

BURNS W. ROPER: In terms of the effect of presidential approval ratings on the public, I might report an experiment we conducted recently. We used a split-sample on one study.* On half of the sample we asked our standard question about whether the respondent was a "Carter supporter" or a "Carter critic." On the other half of the sample we introduced the question by saying, "As you know, all of the polls have been showing support for President Carter going down. We'd like to get your opinion about him." We then went into our regular question. We got only one percentage point difference between the two forms of the question. The difference was in the expected direction, but it still was only one point.

B. FRANK BROWN**: Can interpreting presidential popularity poll results be compared to the reading of tea leaves?

IRVING CRESPI: It depends on how you use presidential popularity. If you use it as an indicator of what will happen in the year ahead, then it's reading tea leaves. If you see the measure in the context of how many people know about the president, have any concept of what he is like, and—among

---

* A "split-sample" is one that is divided into two or more equal and comparable parts. This technique is used by opinion researchers among other things to test the effect of question-wording by asking different variations of a common question at the same time to comparable and similarly designed samples of respondents.

** Charles F. Kettering Foundation.

those who do—what his standing is and why, then you can use it as one datum among many to understand analytically what the current political situation is. This is not reading tea leaves. But, unfortunately, most of the time presidential popularity is used—reported—as tea-leaves reading.

HAROLD WOLMAN*: Isn't one possible explanation for the difference in poll results that when we talk about a poll sample of 1,500, with a sampling error of plus or minus three percentage points, we also refer to a specific level of confidence? For example, if the possible error is within three percentage points 95 percent of the time, five percent of the time the error may be greater and we don't know how much greater. In other words, one poll out of twenty is going to be wrong by more than three percentage points—maybe wildly wrong. This may be what happened before the Republican Convention in 1964 when Nelson Rockefeller was running against Richard Nixon. There was a tremendous discrepancy in Rockefeller-Nixon voter preference polls. It may have been one of those one out of twenty shots for in the next couple of days they were right back where they had been before.

IRVING CRESPI: As the number of polls increases, we ought to be alert to the possibility you mention. At the same time, we ought to remember that sources of error—discrepancies between polls—are due to more than just sampling error. Unless you go through all of the factors, you cannot evaluate whether the differences are due to normal sampling variability or whether they could be explained, for example, by questionnaire effect (question-wording, question placement, etc.) by the sample (general public, registered voters, actual voters, etc.) or by other factors.

---

* The Urban Institute.

Journalism or Social Science?

JEFFREY MILSTEIN*: I think there is a dual obligation, for the pollster and survey researcher, on the one hand, and journalists, on the other, to explain the discrepancies to the public. Even if sampling error is reported, measurement errors can be enormous. It is not just a question of wording, but in what context was the interview done? We ought not report overly precise poll results either as pollsters or as journalists. And, secondly, even when we are measuring attitudes, or even if we are measuring intended behavior, we must make it clear that polls are not very good predictors of action.

* Office of Conservation and Solar Energy, Department of Energy.

PART II

Issues Into Percentages

How can public opinion on policy issues be most adequately measured and interpreted, particularly when many issues are complex and likely to be remote to the daily concerns of the public?

As a starting point for the second panel's consideration of this question, Peter D. Hart outlines some ground rules for the formulation of poll questions that hold greatest prospect for reliably tapping the pertinent dimensions of public opinion. The task of constructing a survey questionnaire ranges from high art—manifest in the trained intuition of how best to frame a series of questions on a complex subject—to a mundane preoccupation with the nuts and bolts of questionnaire design. Hart describes how a seasoned pollster must operate on both levels simultaneously.

To mitigate against discussion at an exclusively general level, two case studies examine the quality of opinion research on two current policy issues: the accident at Three Mile Island and the Strategic Arms Limitation Treaty. Robert Cameron Mitchell and William J. Lanouette, two sympathetic but disinterested observers, summarize existing poll data on the topics, each critiquing the adequacy and contribution of those data to the policy debate.

One consequence of burgeoning polling initiatives across the country is the growing political importance of summary interpretations of diverse poll findings about policy issues. Written by political scientists, journalists, and proponents of one point of view or another, these analyses often contribute crucial synthesis for those within government. On occasion, however, for reasons of enthusiasm or insufficient expertise, these analyses become rhetorical exercises. Everett Carll Ladd, Jr. addresses this problem and discusses some of the pitfalls and potential in the secondary analysis of existing poll data.

All too often deliberations about polling and policy are confined to exchanges between pollsters, journalists, and politicians. Yet, there is perhaps no more "policy-relevant" form of opinion research than consumer and market research. Therefore, Martin Weinberger brings to bear the perspective of consumer research on the question of how opinion research can better contribute to public policy.

AHC

The Art
of Asking Questions*

THE REASON I was asked to participate in this conference, I am sure, was my success in 1978 in "the art of asking questions" when I went out in the state of Iowa and asked the people, "How big do you think Dick Clark will win?" As you know, he didn't win quite as big as we thought he might.

It is difficult in these brief remarks to outline the many considerations bearing on question wording and questionnaire design. What I would like to do is discuss seven of the most important factors we feel should be taken into account in questionnaire design, particularly in polling for candidates for public office.

The first thing, obviously, is statement of goals. Whether these goals are focused enough for the poll to work is up to both the client and the survey research firm. Too many questionnaires tend to be interesting but unenlightening. A candidate has to know what he wants from a survey, and how he will use the information. One of the biggest problems is differentiating between interesting information and strategic information. Whenever a client says to me at the end of a session, "Gee, that was really interesting," I know I have failed, because we are not trying to provide "interesting" information. We are different from newspapers; we are trying to come up with a strategy and direction for a campaign.

Related to goal-setting is deciding how the information will be used. The important point here is that, in terms of questionnaire design, there has to be a definite goal or a

---

* I take the liberty of using the title of Stanley Payne's classic book on questionnaire design (*The Art of Asking Questions,* Princeton University Press, 1951).

structure, and that really comes from our original meeting with the candidate and the insights we get. If the candidate—and it has happened to all pollsters—says: "Look, you are the experts, you go write a questionnaire," it always turns out to be a failure, because the candidate doesn't give you the insights you need. All of us can write a questionnaire about any state without ever bothering to meet with a client, but we are not going to write a sensitive instrument about that state.

The second element of a good questionnaire is creativity—that is, how you get at a question. For example, sometimes to get at a particularly sensitive question, you have to use what I would call the bias of the respondent to get rid of the bias. Let me explain. In 1973, we worked for a lady by the name of Ella Grasso, who was a congresswoman from Connecticut interested in becoming the governor of Connecticut. She asked me two parts of one question: "How do people feel about having a woman as governor? How much bias is there against a woman governor?" That was really basically *all* she asked of me. Now, today we're dealing with certain situations which are probably somewhat akin—the question of Chappaquiddick—and my theory is that it cannot be measured directly but instead must be approached obliquely.

Let me give you an example of how we dealt with the question of bias against a woman governor. We started off asking the voters this question: "There has been a great deal of discussion about women and their role in politics. I am going to read to you a number of different positions in government and for each I would like you to tell me if you feel, in general, this position would be better handled by a man or a woman or would it make no difference?" We led with the head of the FBI. We followed it with the Connecticut attorney general, the head of consumer affairs, the state highway patrol, the Connecticut secretary of state (a position held by Ella Grasso and Gloria Schafer), and only last did we ask about the governor of Connecticut. Why? In essence, what we were trying to do is to say: "Bias is permissible. Sure, some positions are better held by men and some positions are better held by women." By doing this, we found that 39 percent of the voters in Connecticut felt that the governorship was viewed as better held by a man.

We next asked an open-ended question: "What are the advantages and disadvantages of a woman governor?" Finally, we asked: "I would like to read you a list of reasons people have given us why it might not be advisable to have a woman as governor of Connecticut. For each reason, would you tell me in general if you feel that this would be a major problem, a minor problem, or no problem at all?" We included reasons such as: "a woman wouldn't understand the economy"; "a woman would tend to react with emotion not reason"; "a woman would have too many family responsibilities"; "a woman could not command the respect of male officials"; "a woman would give in too easily to confrontation"; "a woman would lack toughness and guts"; "a woman wouldn't be able to inspire people" (the anti-Joan of Arc theory); "a woman would lack courage and strength in a crisis"; "a woman would spend too much money on social programs"; "a woman would be too indecisive"; "a woman would lack the stamina to do the job"; "Connecticut would lose prestige to other states"; "businessmen would not locate in Connecticut"; and "men would try to take advantage of a woman governor."

The point I am trying to make is that the way you approach a problem really tells you how you are going to be able to deal with it. In this instance, what we discovered was that people with the bias were Ella's own peer group—women over fifty. They were reflecting their own values and lifestyles. The two greatest problems they had were that (1) a woman would not be respected by men, and (2) a woman should be raising a family—or would have too many family responsibilities. By understanding what the bias was among this group, we could devise a campaign strategy to deal with it. Ella was elected.

Let's go on to the next element of questionnaire design, which is placement. Placement of questions can really determine what the results of asking a question will be. Polls, which are scientifically conducted, can produce different answers solely as a result of placement. The results can provide the candidate with information which might cause him or her to take some action to deal with a problem, and if the results are biased because of poor placement of the question, the action might be ill-advised. In 1978, we did a poll for Charles Ravenel in South Carolina in which we had him trailing Strom Thurmond by 53 to 39 percent about a month-and-a-half out. That was not exactly good news for Charles Ravenel, but the opponent's pollster had our candidate further behind at the same time: 59 to 23. He was calling my poll bogus, and I felt bad, wondering how I could be that far off. Jim Perry phoned me from the *Wall Street Journal* and said: "Don't worry about it." Strom Thurmond made his poll available, and what they had done was very interesting. They asked a series of negative questions about Charles Ravenel. "Is he too liberal?" "Too much like Kennedy?" "Does it bother you that he spent more of his adult life in New York?" "Does it bother you that he is getting money from Italian businessmen out of New Jersey?" A whole series of questions. Then they said: "Now we would like to ask you how you would vote if the election were held today. Would you vote for Charles Ravenel, the Democrat, or Strom Thurmond, the Republican?" This last question was absolutely fair and unbiased. It was the place that created the bias. The election results were 55-45, which is still a loss, but a little different from 59-23.

Another thing about placement: It's important to work from the general questions to the specific. That is the only way you can do a good poll. This also suggests that open-ended questions of a general nature always come before closed-ended questions. In a political poll, questions making pointed references to political figures should be at the very end of the questionnaire so that they don't bias any questions.

The fourth aspect of a good questionnaire has to do with the range of options you give a respondent. All too often we look at public opinion polls and everything either turns out to be black or white; everybody agrees or everybody disagrees with a particular statement. The fact of the matter is that even though there may be a whole range of opinions, they tend to be forced into a two-part dichotomy. This is particularly a problem with closed-ended questions. They can be terribly misleading because the respondents are forced to give choices that do not reflect their total opinion. Obviously, if I asked you to choose between A and B, I can force you to indicate a preference, but your opinion may be somewhere in the middle, or your opinion might be much broader than the choices given.

You see this problem in a series of agree-disagree statements, always a favorite with members of the press. Why? Because the statements are black and white. (We use these kinds of questions in our private polling, but for a different purpose: we are trying to figure out how far you can press an advantage.) For example, an agree-disagree question might be built around the statement: "The oil companies are doing all they can to help solve energy problems, and should not be criticized so much." By changing a couple of words the entire meaning of the results could change. Or, another kind of question: "Now I am going to read you a list of names, and for each, tell me whether you have a generally favorable or unfavorable impression." There is no neutral option given; if everybody has to be categorized as having a favorable or unfavorable impression you can have problems because opinion is not that narrow.

Next is the matter of balance. I often say that we are

sometimes like sculptors, or a person who does mobiles. You can look at a mobile, and say that the artist did a good job or he didn't do a good job. You don't have to be an expert in the field. All you have to do is go into a gallery, and you say "This isn't hanging right." If you stop and look at a questionnaire, instead of just the results, you should say, "Does this balance?" or "Is this really fair?" I guarantee that in practically every survey that Hart Research does we err on balance. It is just so hard because you look at the wording, and you think you've structured it just right. It comes back, and you realize that the question was loaded. One of my rules is that if any answer comes back 70-15 or above, either it is a poor question, or you had no right to ask it in the first place. A good question is well-balanced: It gives an opportunity for a full range of opinion so everybody will feel comfortable finding a place.

The sixth element of good questionnaire design relates to a number of the other points I have made: the importance of impartiality. In political polling, impartiality means that you have not tried to load up favorable things for your candidate. If we deliver good news to our clients and it is not accurate, we are out of business. I know there is always the feeling that somehow we are in an advocacy position, trying to give our clients better news. The fact is that we have got to tell it like it is. It is the same as being a doctor. You can't say the results are better than they are. Whatever the numbers are, we want to get the fairest and most accurate reflection of the electorate.

Finally, let me talk about meticulousness. In our business, we take six hundred people to represent a state or fifteen hundred people to represent the nation. Everybody can draw a good sample, or can work on one aspect of polling or another; but the actual meticulousness and the way information is presented—both to the respondent and to the interviewer—makes a big difference in the results you get. The point is that it is very important to be precise. If a questionnaire isn't precise or if the interviewer has great flexibility in what he or she is doing, you've got problems because that means you've got fifty people in the field doing fifty different things.

Questionnaire design is such an important part of our business that I have gone over it in a fair amount of detail. You will find that the results of a survey are no better than the questionnaire.

Robert Cameron Mitchell

Polling on Nuclear Power:
A Critique of the Polls After Three Mile Island

PUBLIC POLLS on issues can serve three useful functions. First, they can be "event assessors" by documenting the public's reaction to events such as Three Mile Island, the capture of the Mayaguez, or a debate between presidential candidates. Second, polls can serve as "temperature takers" on long-standing issues. By repeating key questions over time, such as, "Should we build more nuclear power plants?" or, "Do you approve or disapprove of the way Jimmy Carter is handling his job as president?" polls can monitor the shifts in public opinion on an issue or a political figure just as a doctor monitors the course of a patient's fever. The third function, that of "issue clarifier," is by far the most important. Polls have the capacity to clarify issues by ascertaining people's knowledge about an issue, probing why they hold the views they hold, and identifying which policy solutions people prefer and why. An issue such as abortion can be clarified in part by identifying the conditions under which people believe that abortions should or should not be permitted, and the extent to which people support such current policy options as a constitutional convention to consider the issue or the prohibition of government medicaid funds for abortion.

Because it was a major news event and part of an already existing national controversy, the accident at Three Mile Island was the focus of considerable public opinion polling.[1] The accident began in the early morning of Wednesday,

March 28, 1979, and the hydrogen bubble danger was declared over on Monday, April 2, the day after the President's visit. By April 3, the *Washington Post* was in the field with a regional survey*, followed by CBS/New York Times and the first of Harris's three immediate post-TMI surveys[2] on April 4, Cambridge Reports on April 6, and Gallup on April 7. These were substantial polls: The number of questions on nuclear power ranged from 11 in the Gallup survey to a grand total of 37 in the second ABC/Harris survey. In succeeding months polling on the nuclear power issue continued, albeit with many further questions per survey.

Looking just at the publicly available polls (no doubt a fair amount of polling on this issue was also conducted for corporate clients during this period, but these polls are unavailable to me), I count a total of at least thirteen national and eight state or regional polls which asked more than 150 different questions (Mitchell, 1979b). The following critique is based on these data and the news articles which reported them. I conclude that on the issue of nuclear power the polls functioned best as event assessors. As temperature takers they performed fairly well, although there is considerable room for improvement. The most serious weaknesses lie in the area of issue clarification.

Assessment of the Three Mile Island Accident

The polls' handling of the accident at Three Mile Island was very good on the whole. They waited until the imminent danger caused by the fear of a hydrogen bubble explosion was over before beginning their polling. Once in the field they did extensive surveys, often repeating questions for trend purposes which they had asked in earlier surveys and which I will discuss in the next section. Obviously some

---

* An index to the polls referred to will be found in the appendix on page 93.

polls did a better job of covering the important questions than others, but in the aggregate we have a useful picture of the public's assessment of the event. Where topics have been covered by more than one poll the results are reassuringly consistent.

Instead of taking the public's awareness of the accident for granted, several polls specifically asked people whether they had heard of the accident (75 percent, 96 percent and 90 percent in three surveys had). Only one poll asked people how serious they felt the accident was, but two others measured how "disturbed" or "worried about self or family's safety" people were as a result of the accident. A clear picture emerges of considerable public concern. By presenting a regional breakdown Gallup showed that personal safety fears were much higher in the East.

A crucial issue in evaluating the effect of TMI on the public's acceptance of nuclear power is the extent to which people wrote it off as a freak occurrence or viewed it as a harbinger of the future. Four polls asked about this and several of the questions were exceptionally well phrased. Depending on the question wording, percentages ranging from 50 to 75 in three national and one regional poll (CBS 1, Harris 1, Gallup 1, WP 1) said that TMI was not a freak occurrence.

With generally consistent results, several polls probed the public's evaluation of how well the major actors at TMI "handled" the situation and how candid they were in their public statements. The CBS/New York Times Poll went a step further, however, and asked their respondents whether they thought public officials "should keep back information if they're afraid people will panic." Thirty-eight percent agreed with this notion. This suggests that it would be wrong to assume that all of the 41 percent in a Roper poll who believed the "nuclear regulatory spokesman" concealed the danger that existed at Three Mile Island necessarily disapproved of the concealment.

A related issue of considerable importance is the public's evaluation of the media's handling of the accident. The plant did not blow up, after all, nor was anyone physically injured (as far as we know) despite the crisis portrayed in the newspapers and on television. Did people feel the media had misled them about the severity of the accident? Unfortunately, only three polls asked questions about this. According to a nationwide and state poll taken right after the accident, 28 percent felt that the media had blown the accident up out of proportion (CBS 1) and 40 percent in the Western states regarded newspaper, TV, and radio coverage as "basically opinionated and emotional" (Rocky). A poll taken in late June found that 25 percent believed "most of the press" exaggerated the danger involved at the time (Roper 1). The wording of this question is ambiguous, however,[3] so we really don't have any valid after-the-fact assessment of the press coverage.[4]

Temperature Taking on Nuclear Power's Acceptability to the Public

The fundamental question raised by the accident at TMI, of course, is what effect it would have on public support for nuclear power in general. As early as three years ago Alvin Weinberg declared that the "most serious question now facing nuclear energy is its acceptance by the public." Would the accident at TMI cause a major shift in opinion against nuclear power since it appeared to confirm some of its critics' most harsh accusations?

Short of conducting a panel study in which the same people are interviewed repeatedly, the best way to measure shifts in public sentiment on an issue like nuclear power is to use trend data where the same questions are asked of comparable samples at different times. Here the polls did quite well. Because a number of the survey organizations have been polling on nuclear energy for years they were able to and did repeat key questions from these earlier surveys in their post-TMI polls. Moreover, both Harris and Cambridge Reports have asked one particular question with such regularity over the years that it provides a particularly useful trend line. This question is: "In general, do you favor or oppose the building of more nuclear power plants in the United States?"

The Harris and Cambridge results, shown in Figure 1, reveal that although the accident did result in a significant increase in public opposition, support for nuclear energy did not by any means collapse as some of its opponents had anticipated. Although they had only one or two pre-TMI nuclear polls to draw on, CBS/New York Times and Gallup also reported similar trends. In every post-TMI poll except two of Cambridge's, pluralities still favored building more nuclear power plants. CBS and Gallup also asked a second trend question about building nuclear power plants "in your community" or "within five miles of here." The responses showed large shifts in opinion from the earlier 1975 and 1977 polls, with strong majorities in the post-TMI polls opposing the construction of local plants.

The interpreter of these trend results faces the classic is-the-glass-half-full-or-half-empty dilemma. Does one emphasize the sharp rise in opposition or the fact that the bottom did not fall out of nuclear's support? Here are the relevant headlines from the pollsters' press releases showing how they handled this dilemma:

Harris release April 26, 1979:
AMERICANS OPPOSE PERMANENTLY CLOSING
ALL NUCLEAR POWER PLANTS
DESPITE THREE MILE ISLAND ACCIDENT

Harris release May 3, 1979:
AMERICANS UNWILLING TO DECLARE A
MORATORIUM ON NUCLEAR POWER, DESPITE
INCREASING WORRIES ABOUT ITS SAFETY

Gallup Index April, 1979:
AMERICANS FAVOR 'GO-SLOW' APPROACH
BUT CONTINUE TO FAVOR NUCLEAR POWER

CBS/New York Times release April 9, 1979:
ONLY SLIGHT MARGIN OF APPROVAL
NOW RUNNING FOR BUILDING MORE
NUCLEAR POWER PLANTS... NUCLEAR POWER
CLEAR CHOICE OVER HIGH PRICED OIL
(summary statements on cover of release).

New York Times story April 10, 1979:
POLL SHOWS SHARP RISE SINCE '77
IN OPPOSITION TO NUCLEAR PLANTS

Each of these headlines summarizes the overall findings of the poll which was being reported, of course, but the trend data were (or should have been) a centerpiece to the story. The *New York Times'* story was much more a "half-empty" interpretation than the early Harris release, but the CBS/ NYTimes survey included the plant-in-your-community question, which Harris did not. Conversely, Harris included a shut-existing-plants-down question (only a few supported this policy) which the CBS/NYTimes survey did not. On the whole each of these interpretations is defensible in the context of its poll's findings. Moreover, the releases discuss both the pro- and anti-nuclear findings with appropriate care.

In summary, the polls did use trend data and they interpreted the results without undue bias. Nevertheless, there were some weaknesses in the reporting of the principal trend data, the method of presenting trend data in the press is primitive and needs to be improved, and the basic trend question itself is far too simplistic an indicator. Three weaknesses are particularly noteworthy.

The first is the case of the apparently new data point and the case of the missing data point.* ABC/Harris and

---

* Poll results at a given point in time.

Cambridge Reports have monitored public opinion on nuclear power over a number of years. Of these only the ABC/Harris trend is publicly reported. Harris is to be commended for the depth of its polling on the nuclear issue and for making a relatively long term trend available to the public. No doubt it was for these reasons that Mark Schulman, a Harris vice-president, was invited by *Public Opinion* magazine to write an article interpreting the public response to TMI. In his article (Schulman, 1979a), Schulman used substantially the Harris trend line shown in Figure 1. Its ups and downs, he argued, show that people are crisis-oriented and that opinion on nuclear power fluctuates in response to the headlines. I have no quarrel with this interpretation in its weak form[5] and later Harris polling has confirmed the validity of his generalization. His response-to-the-headlines interpretation of the trend depends on one key data point, however, the one marked A on Figure 1 for April 1976, which shows a sharp dip to a 44 percent support level. Without this dip the trend line would show only a gradual decline in support over the years prior to TMI; with it we have Schulman's "roller coaster" effect. In an earlier version of this paper I questioned this sudden emergence of a previously unreleased[6] data point (which was apparently part of a proprietary poll) at a much later time when its release appeared to be in the interests of the Harris poll's clients in the nuclear industry. I now understand (Schulman, 1979b) that Harris had cleared the release of the full trend including this data point in the winter of 1979, well before Three Mile Island, although the release was unavoidably delayed because of the accident. It is regrettable that the 1976 data point's release was delayed for so long as it adds a great deal to our understanding of the Harris trend line, but the Harris organization is to be commended for its effort in obtaining release of data gathered on this subject for its private clients.[7]

In the original version I also expressed puzzlement that

FIGURE 1

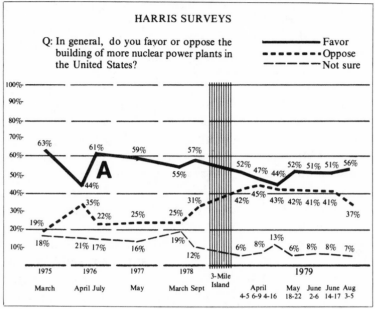

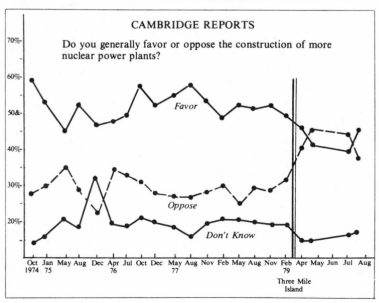

the Harris organization would fail to replicate the having-nuclear-plant-in-your-community question in any of its several publicly reported post-TMI surveys. After all, they had asked this question in 1975 and 1976, and Schulman's article reported its use in a now-released study (in which majorities rejected a local nuclear power plant for the first time) conducted in October 1978 to substantiate his claim that the shift against local plants occurred *before* TMI. Surely this question should have been a prime candidate for a post-TMI trend especially in conjunction with an excellent companion question, also asked in the October 1978 Harris poll, about having a coal-fired plant in the respondents' community (which was also rejected by approximately the same margin). According to Schulman, this question was not asked after the Three Mile Island accident because the CBS / New York Times polls had already asked it and it didn't seem worth while to repeat the question again. However, Harris mounted two long surveys (a phone survey on April 6-9 with 28 questions and a personal interview survey on April 4-16 with 13 questions on nuclear power) before the results of the relevant CBS/New York Times poll of April 5-7 were made public. Consequently, I still don't understand why this question was omitted from these lengthy surveys and believe that if Harris had asked both it and the parallel question about a local coal-fired plant at that time, the results would have added much to our understanding of the public's response to the accident.

A second weakness worth calling attention to is found in the way trend data are reported.

The fever chart shown at the foot of hospital beds in old films is just that, a chart. Instead of a string of numbers, it graphically shows the course of the patient's temperature by use of a single line. Why is it that every newspaper report on the nuclear trend data simply repeats a string of numbers when it would be far easier for readers to understand the trends if they were shown on a chart? Swedish newspapers have done exactly this in reporting the latest trends in opinion on nuclear power.

A third weakness is what seems to be one of the unspoken rules of contemporary polling on the issues: Never give a respondent the chance to say he or she doesn't have an opinion on the issue. The build-more-nuclear-plants question certainly does not offer such an option: The respondent is asked simply whether he or she favors or opposes such plants. Some respondents still refuse to conform, of course, and are counted as "don't know." It seems to me that this approach badly distorts the reality of public opinion on issues such as nuclear energy. It is far more reasonable to assume that many people really don't have an opinion on such issues or are uncertain. If this is the case then it would be helpful to know how large this group of people is and who they are. Consider the following data from two of Barry Sussman's *Washington Post* surveys:

Washington Post Regional Poll/April 3-6, 1979

If someone asked before last week's accident in Penn-sylvania, would you have described yourself as a supporter of nuclear power plants, an opponent of nuclear power plants, or neutral on power plants? How about now?		Before (Retrospective)	After
	A supporter	38%	38%
	Neutral and/or not sure	44%	34%
	An opponent	18%	28%

Washington Post National Poll/May 3-17, 1979

Would you describe yourself as a supporter of nuclear power plants as a means of providing electricity, an opponent of nuclear power plants, or haven't you made up your mind?	Supporter	36%
	Opponent	26%
	Uncertain	38%

His findings—that at least a third of the public is neutral on the issue of nuclear power—confirm some of my own polling results. By adding the right kinds of follow-up questions to a question like this which legitimates the expression of uncertainty, much more useful information can be obtained. One sequence for revised trend questions would run as follows:

(1) In general, do you favor or oppose building more nuclear power plants in the United States or haven't you made up your mind on the issue?

IF RESPONDENT HASN'T MADE UP MIND
(1a) Which way do you lean at this time? Do you lean toward favoring the building of more nuclear power plants or do you lean against building more?

IF RESPONDENT HAS MADE UP MIND
(1b) How strongly do you feel about this issue? Are you strongly in favor (opposed) to building more nuclear plants or don't you feel that strongly about it?

The end result would be seven categories of people ranging from strong supporters of building more plants to strong opponents, with a neutral middle category. Trends based on these categories would vastly expand our knowledge about public acceptance of nuclear power.[8]

Clarifying the Nuclear Issue

As a way of clarifying the nuclear issue, the polls fell far short of their potential. Admittedly, the nuclear issue presents the pollster with a major challenge: Not only does it involve a complex technology based on scientific principles about which most of the public only knows a few clichés, but nuclear power itself is just one of a number of energy supply and demand options, each of which has its complexities and uncertainties. The answer to the question of whether we should build more nuclear power plants, therefore, hinges on the respondent's views about both nuclear safety and the availability of other energy options. Even within the limitations of asking only a relatively small number of questions on the issue, however, much more can be done to clarify the nature of the nuclear debate and the policy options people prefer and why they prefer them.

1. Nature of the debate. The extent to which an issue is salient to people can vary enormously. What percent are really personally concerned about nuclear power? With the exception of one CBS/NYTimes survey (CBS/NYT 2) which asked people whether a candidate's position against nuclear power would make them more or less likely to vote for him or her (43 percent said more, 26 percent said less) none of the post-TMI polls asked people how much they personally cared about the issue or how important it was to them.

The debate over nuclear power includes several important sub-issues. Nuclear energy is criticized variously for: a) the lack of a solution to the nuclear waste problem; b) the undue probability of a melt-down; c) the extent of the low-level radiation emissions associated with the technology; d) the dangers associated with transporting nuclear materials to and from plants and reprocessing and waste storage facilities; e) the technology's contribution to nuclear proliferation; f) the technology's contribution to centralized government and economic structure; g) the prospect of a "police state" to guard the technology, and so on. An understanding of the public's views on the issue would be greatly aided by knowing which of these problems is of most concern but only one post-TMI poll—a Harris poll (Harris 2) which asked about waste disposal, low-level radioactivity, and safety—sought people's views on these sub-problems.

The nuclear energy issue is one about which the "experts" quoted in the press hold many different views. What does the public actually know about the nuclear energy issue? What percent know roughly how many plants are in operation or are planned, or approximately what proportion of our electricity is produced by nuclear power? Which experts do they trust, if any? Only CBS/NYTimes and Harris asked questions which might be said to measure people's knowledge on the issue, and the wording of the Harris questions is ambiguous.[9] No poll asked people directly how well informed they felt they were on the issue. Nor were people asked how much confidence they have in the national agency which is regulating nuclear power, the power companies who are building and running the plants, or the groups who are opposing the building of the plants.

Finally, the nuclear energy issue has been brought to national attention by a set of challengers who are loosely referred to as the anti-nuclear movement. With the exception of two polling organizations whose findings are prepared for the use of their private subscribers (Cambridge and Opinion Research Corporation),[10] no poll asked people for their views about the movement or about the movement's proposals.

2. Policy Options. The question of policy options in the nuclear issue involves two major dimensions. First, nuclear power is one of several ways of meeting our energy needs. Any understanding of people's views on the issue requires an understanding of how they evaluate nuclear power in comparison with the most important alternatives. Second, several different policies can be taken with regard to nuclear power itself, ranging from immediately abandoning the technology to going ahead with it in its present form. Polls did not pose the most relevant alternatives in a clear manner on either of these dimensions.

With regard to the alternatives to nuclear energy, the

polls concentrated on supply alternatives far more than the demand alternatives such as conservation or cutting back (CBS 1 and WISC were the only exceptions), and within the supply alternatives they emphasized the alternatives of oil (at increased prices or dependence on foreign nations), coal, or the "possibility of shortages" (Gallup), and ignored questions which offered the alternative of nuclear vs. renewable energy sources. I have no quarrel with asking questions comparing nuclear with higher prices, coal, and the possibility of shortages. I do think the so-called "soft energy path" which is at the center of the energy debate *also* deserves careful study, especially when some respected experts such as the Harvard Business School energy study group (Yergin, 1979) and the Institute for Energy Analysis (Whittle, 1979) suggest that a nuclear moratorium may not necessarily entail much in the way of higher prices or shortages.

The wording of the questions that posed energy alternatives were unsatisfactory for the most part. Rarely were the other energy alternatives systematically compared with nuclear and all too often a single question arbitrarily included two or even three dimensions, making it impossible to separate out which of those dimensions was influencing the respondent's answer.

Posing different policy options with regard to nuclear power itself should have been an easier task than designing the comparison questions, yet the same failure occurred here as well. The national polls all adopted the technique of posing policy options as separate questions instead of the more straightforward technique of asking the respondent to choose one of an array of mutually incompatible options. Thus some national polls asked people if they wanted to close down all plants; almost every one asked whether we should build more; and, in its April 6-9 survey, the ABC/ Harris poll explored a range of options including a temporary moratorium until safety problems are resolved and allowing the plants that are presently planned to be built with the government supervising their construction "more strictly than has been the case up to now." By perusing all these polls it is possible to piece together a picture of the relative support for the various options from these separate questions, and I have done this in my own research (Mitchell, 1979a).

The direct strategy of asking people which *one* policy option they prefer was only used by four of the state polls. Unfortunately, none of these questions was fully satisfactory. Instead of simply proposing discrete alternatives most of these polls made them contingent on safety assurances, thereby introducing a confounding variable, and none of them posed the policy alternative that the plants already under construction should be finished but no more plants should be planned.[11]

3. Why do people hold the views they do? The public polls typically do not pretend to present in-depth analysis of issues, nor is it reasonable to expect them to. Nevertheless, in a modest way they do explore the question of why people hold the views they do. This is the case when they ask questions about people's perceptions of the advantages and disadvantages of nuclear power, for example, or when they cross-tabulate regions of the country by worry about the Three Mile Island accident as Gallup did. Even within the public polls' limitations, however, their explanatory efforts leave much to be desired. Here are two examples.

First, it is astonishing that after the accident none of the national polls asked people directly whether or not they believe that nuclear power plants *can be* made sufficiently safe to permit their use. From the evidence on safety that one can glean from the many national questions which mention it in other contexts, a strong majority of the public appears to believe that the technology can be made safe, suggesting that this belief may well be why nuclear continues to enjoy public support. But only the state polls asked this question directly (MA, ROCKY). Here is what the Rocky Mountain Poll found:

Rocky Mountail Poll, ca. April 5-10, 1979[12]

Do you think the safety systems for nuclear power plants can or cannot be perfected enough to prevent accidents such as the one that occurred in Pennsylvania from happening again?	Can	70%
	Cannot	21%
	Not sure	9%

My second example concerns the question of people's acceptance of local nuclear power plants. Even if the public is willing to accept nuclear power in general, opposition to the construction of new plants by large majorities of local residents could prove fatal to the expansion of nuclear energy. At the very least, it would be a strong argument in favor of Alvin Weinberg's proposal that all new plants be sited alongside the existing plants (Weinberg, 1979). As noted above, several post-TMI polls asked about siting and Harris has asked this same question in a series of pre-TMI polls. There are two serious problems with the neighborhood plant questions, however, which make them far less useful than they might be. First, the questions locate the plant "within five miles" or "in your community." Only a small number of people are likely to find themselves living that near a plant even if present siting practices are continued. It would be far more realistic to specify a larger distance of fifteen, or as the Opinion Research Corporation has done in several of its past surveys for the Federal Energy Administration, twenty miles. The second problem is whether those who oppose the siting of a nuclear plant in their vicinity take this position because they are worried about the risks associated with nuclear power or whether they would oppose *any* local power plant no matter what fuel it used. The October 1978 Harris poll cited by Schulman (1979a:7) found people as opposed to a coal-fired plant in their community (by 55-37 percent) as to a nuclear plant (56-33 percent); consequently any further use of the neighborhood nuclear plant question should also pair it with questions about similar non-nuclear plants.

On the whole the public polls do not clarify public issues nearly as well as they might. The reasons for their failure lie in the fact that they are essentially journalistic enterprises. Each of the major TV networks now has its own polling operation (CBS News, NBC Poll) or an arrangement with an outside pollster (ABC/Harris poll). The print media are not far behind. *Time* magazine uses Yankelovich, Skelly and White, the *New York Times* is in partnership with CBS News, and the *Washington Post* commissions its own polls, as do the *Boston Globe* and the *Des Moines Register and Tribune,* among others. Gallup and Harris syndicate their results.

The news media require poll data that are credible, timely, interesting, and *simple* to understand. Credibility is achieved by contracting with reputable pollsters or by conducting polls that are recognized as methodologically sound by reputable pollsters. Timeliness requires getting into the field quickly after a new issue or aspect of an issue (e.g., the accident at Three Mile Island) arises and having a fast turnaround time once the field work has been completed. The criterion that the poll data be of interest to readers or viewers demands that the issues which each poll covers be topical. As a result, public polling for the news media is necessarily broad-brushed with the pollsters measuring opinion on a wide variety of issues. Only rarely, as with the polling on presidential candidates and on energy policy, are more than four or five questions asked on a particular topic by one survey. The concern for simplicity lends itself to dichotomous yes/no, agree/disagree response categories, to the reporting of simple marginal results, and to language which reifies "the public."*

The nature of journalism and the exigencies of journalistic polling lend themselves far more to assessing events than to clarifying issues. To clarify issues properly, considerable time has to be devoted to studying the issue, devising potential questions; pretesting them, and performing multivariate analysis to unravel the causal factors that lie behind the expression of opinion. Public pollsters, however, are forced to jump from one issue to another and to develop questionnaires under great time pressures. Even if they were inclined to undertake detailed analyses of their data, their media clients usually want only the marginals or, at most, clearly understood cross-tabs to present to their viewership or readership. Accordingly the "bottom line" for the public poll is an interesting and plausible story rather than an authoritative explanation of the public's responses.

Given the above, is it a counsel of perfection to criticize the analytical quality of the journalistic public polls on nuclear power? I think not. In the first place, some of the polling firms which are active in public polling, like Harris, also conduct private studies of nuclear power public opinion for clients which involve a larger number of questions than is usually possible in a public poll and include the preparation of an analytical report. The subject expertise they accumulate in this way should make it possible for them to do a better issue-clarifying job in their public polls on nuclear power. Secondly, issues like nuclear power or government spending are not one-shot issues. They have been with us for years and a modest amount of foresight suggests that they will continue to be with us for some time to come. Despite the strictures of journalistic

---

* "Marginals" refer to the overall results to poll questions; "cross-tabs" are the results when the relationship between the pattern of responses to two questions is analyzed.

polling it should not be unreasonable to expect some improvements in question choice and wording.

Even if better analysis is possible, should journalists—whose methods traditionally are concerned with description rather than the social scientists' aim of explanation and prediction—commission polls which meet the social scientists' (and therefore my) criteria? According to Herbert Gans, the media's lay audience (which does not include my fellow social scientists or policymakers for that matter) does not want highly technical "expert news" and cannot reasonably be expected to want such news "until it can also expect to play expert roles and secure the influence, education, and other perquisites that go along with these roles" (Gans, 1979:308). Applying this view to the public polls, a failure to clarify issues would not only be understandable, but also desirable because of the nature of the mass media audience.

While this is a valid argument for leaving detailed studies to the academics and to the pollsters working under contract for a sponsor, it does not apply to the modest improvements that I am suggesting. I suspect the general public would be as interested in questions about support for the anti-nuclear movement and about confidence in government and industry regulation of nuclear power as they were in most of the 150-plus questions that did get asked in the post-accident polls. I think a more coherent analysis highlighting and demonstrating the important role of safety in determining people's support or opposition to nuclear power would interest the public more than the present scatter shot presentation. Certainly the finding that people are as leery of local coal-fired plants as they are of local nuclear plants would be enlightening to many. The improvements in issue-clarification on the nuclear issue which I am suggesting here simply involve the polls doing better what they already do; they will not necessarily entail greater intellectual demands of the readership or viewership. In fact, if James David Barber's critique of the network news is correct (Barber, 1979), it is precisely the least educated viewers and readers who will benefit the most from greater issue clarification.

When it comes to the horse-race aspect of politics, the public polls are thorough and imaginative in probing the relative standings of the various aspirants for the presidency, suggesting both that they are capable of conducting reasonably sophisticated polls and that they believe their constituency is interested in an interpretative analysis of poll data, at least on this topic. So the potential for greater issue-clarification is there; it simply isn't being used. Perhaps James Fallows's recent accusation that "most" reporters lack an interest in the substance of government as opposed to its politics applies equally as well to public polling. Fallows argues that reporters feel comfortable reporting in depth on scandals, internal rivalry, and politicians' gaffes; that they apply their finest analyses to the horse-race aspect of politics, where their judgments are superb; but when it comes to the substance of government, most lack either the interest or the confidence to probe and evaluate.

> In place of appraisal, there is quotation—we get quotes pro and con on each great national issue of the day. In theory this is supposed to equip us to draw our own conclusions; in practice, it denies us the crucial facts necessary for judgment. . . . (Fallows, 1979:16).

Since the public acceptability of nuclear power is an acknowledged factor in the nuclear debate it should not be surprising that the participants in the debate use the results of public opinion polls to make points for their respective arguments. The nuclear industry has undertaken extensive private polling over the years, using Harris and Cambridge (and perhaps other polling firms as well). Those commissioning the three major Harris studies in 1975 (Ebasco Services Incorporated), 1976 (Ebasco), and 1978 (a consortium of companies including Westinghouse, Babcock and Wilcox, and the Edison Electric Institute) authorized their full release and the favorable outcome of these polls was publicized by the Atomic Industrial Forum. Although the opponents of nuclear power command far less resources with which to commission polls than its proponents, they have done so in at least two instances on the state level. In 1978, the New York State Against Jamesport/Shoreham West organization commissioned the Harris organization to do a statewide telephone poll of registered voters in New York. In Wisconsin an environmental group, Wisconsin's Environmental Decade, Inc., had the Wisconsin Survey Research Laboratory do a statewide poll in May 1979. Both polls were well publicized by the sponsoring groups, who regarded their findings as favorable to their cause. The groups also released the complete results of their polls to those who requested them.

The accident at Three Mile Island raised the anti-nuclear movement's hopes for increased public support while those in favor of nuclear power were fearful of a strong negative reaction. As it turned out, the polls—like the accident itself—were equivocal, permitting multiple interpretations. For the most part, the actors in the debate used the post-accident poll data with restraint. Opponents of nuclear power like Ralph Nader (*Energy Day,* April 20, 1979) claimed a shift in opinion in their direction. In an article addressed to their anti-nuclear constituency, Don Michak and Joseph Bowring optimistically declared ". . . the majority of Americans [are] moving to oppose further nuclear development," (Michak and Bowring, 1979:8). For its part, industry did not minimize the decline in support but emphasized the continuing plurality in support of building more plants and other results which showed strong public opposition to shutting down plants already in operation.

The Atomic Industrial Forum also publicized the Harris trend results for May-August 1979 which showed a partial but significant recovery in support.

Conclusion

Despite the rancorous conflict which has become increasingly associated with questions of the risks and benefits of nuclear power, the polls on nuclear energy, with the exception of the case described in the Addendum, have served far more as a source of useful information than as a source of confusion. Likewise, press coverage of the nuclear polls has avoided sensationalism or egregious misinterpretations. The real problem with the post-Three Mile Island polling on the nuclear issue is that both the polling and the media analysis of the poll results are far more superficial than they need to be. The public deserves better polling on this (and other) issues.

Addendum

At the time of the conference I knew of no public misuse of the polls on nuclear power by the protagonists in the nuclear debate. This stood in sharp contrast to the polling on SALT. On December 4, 1979, however, the use of the poll data in the nuclear debate took a new turn. On that date, the American Nuclear Energy Council placed a two-page ad in the *Washington Post* which vigorously advocated the further development of nuclear energy and opposed a "moratorium" (see Figure 2). One of the major arguments set forth in the ad asserted that "public opinion opposed a moratorium." Its poorly documented use of public opinion data is wrong in two respects and misleading in another and raises a question about how much obligation polling organizations—in this case Cambridge Reports—have to make proprietary polls public when they have been misinterpreted by clients to the public.

The erroneous statements in the ad are:

- *"All* (boldface type in the original) national surveys have shown the American public consistently supporting nuclear power over the years."

COMMENT: This is not the case for the post-accident Cambridge trend data on page 73. Other questions which do not support this generalization include those about having a nuclear power plant in your community and tradeoff questions which show (after the accident) that people would far prefer coal to nuclear (66 to 25 percent) or cutting back their own use of energy to nuclear (68 to 25 percent).[13]

- "Following Three Mile Island, the level of support dipped, but supporters of nuclear energy still heavily outnumber those who want to halt its development."

COMMENT: The Cambridge trend line, to which this statement seems to refer, does not show supporters "heavily outnumbering" opponents following the accident. In the Cambridge poll immediately preceding Three Mile Island, those wanting to build more nuclear plants outnumbered those opposed by 50 to 32 percent—an 18 point margin. Perhaps, by stretching the finding, this margin of support might justify the ad's claim. But *following* the accident the Cambridge polls show a decline in the margin of support to 7 percent (April 1979) and 9 percent (July/ August 1979), the latest data point available to the writers of the ad.

- "With a majority of Americans already opposed to a moratorium, just how popular will a moratorium be when brownouts occur, factories and schools are closed, gasoline lines reappear, homes are cold in the winter, and prices continue to soar?"

COMMENT: This statement appears after a series of four poll results which are attributed to Cambridge Reports, Inc. (with no information about the date of the poll, the sample, the method of polling, the sponsor or the actual text of the question). Two of the cited results are relevant to the assertion that a majority of the public opposes a moratorium. One result shows 68 percent oppose closing down the existing plants and the second has 51 percent opposing a halt in the construction of new plants. My concern here lies in the definition of "moratorium." Various kinds of moratoria have been proposed and some of these were indeed rejected in post-accident polls such as Cambridge's. Those that were not rejected, however, include the type of temporary *de facto* moratorium which the Nuclear Regulatory Commission had imposed following the accident and the short-term moratorium proposed by Rep. Edward J. Markey (D-Mass.) which Congress was considering at the time of the ad's placement.[14] Since the ad is directed to "the President & Congress" it would appear that it is this type of

Portion of a two page ad in the *Washington Post,* December 4, 1979, sponsored by the American Nuclear Energy Council:

A MESSAGE TO THE PRESIDENT & CONGRESS: AMERICA'S NEED FOR NUCLEAR POWER.... AND HOW WE ARE MAKING IT SAFER

PUBLIC OPINION OPPOSES A MORATORIUM

Before making final judgment on the future of nuclear power, Congress and the President should also consider the following facts: All national surveys have shown the American public consistently supporting nuclear power over the years. Following Three Mile Island, the level of support dipped, but supporters of nuclear energy still heavily outnumber those who want to halt its development.

For Example:*

- 68% of the American public oppose closing down existing nuclear power plants; only 17% favor such a drastic step.
- 51% oppose a policy that would allow only current plants to operate while construction of new plants is halted; only 33% favor such a moratorium.
- 61% agree with this statement: "In spite of the fact that Three Mile Island occurred, America still needs more energy in the future and nuclear power must continue to be one of our sources of energy."
- Most importantly, all of the surveys show that public support for nuclear power increases in direct proportion to America's need for energy, even though they recognize there are safety risks.

The political question to consider is this: With a majority of Americans already opposed to a moratorium, just how popular will a moratorium be when brownouts occur, factories and schools are closed, gasoline lines reappear, homes are cold in the winter, and prices continue to soar?

Only a policy of conservation and increasing energy supplies will lead America out of the energy crisis.

* Polling information supplied by Cambridge Reports, Inc.

moratorium that is most relevant to the ad's argument. An examination of the actual wording of the Cambridge questions shows that they do *not* refer to this type of temporary moratorium, which is intended to be lifted once the safety changes necessitated by the Three Mile Island accident are defined and implemented. Furthermore, other polls about this issue have found that large majorities were actually in favor of this kind of halt.[15]

Having documented the misrepresentation and the outright error in the American Nuclear Energy Council's ad, what interests me most is not that the Council misused the poll data but the extent to which the polling organization which supplied the data did not feel accountable for correcting their misuse. Along with other reputable polling organizations, Cambridge Reports reserves the right to correct public releases of the data it collects for proprietary clients. Naturally, the client has the right to keep the results of a study it pays for confidential if it so chooses. If the client releases any portion of the data, however, Cambridge Reports has a contractual right to correct the public release of erroneous data or analyses "by the release of the correct information or such other measures as may be needed."[16] Such a policy has the potential to preserve the reputation of polling organizations and the quality of the policy debate because clients who know that a partial release of their data is going to obligate them to its full release are likely to avoid egregious misrepresentation of the data. Since the ad appeared when I was revising this paper for publication and since it is to my knowledge the major misuse of poll data to date in the nuclear debate, I used it as a test case of how well this admirable self-policing policy works in practice.

I made a written request for the "report of the survey(s) from which these data [those referred to in the ad] were derived, which give the findings for all the questions used in the relevant survey for the client, the question wording, the question sequence, and information about the timing and sample size of the survey." This request for the entire set of survey results was based on my view that only knowing the response to all the questions about nuclear power in the survey(s) would give me an adequate basis for evaluating the truth of the ad's claims. A less than complete disclosure of the data would always leave open the question of whether the unreleased data contained findings which contradicted the sponsor's public claims.

Although Cambridge acknowledged that the ad did misrepresent their findings to some extent, they denied my request for full disclosure. The ad had drawn on two surveys which Cambridge conducted after Three Mile Island for a client in the nuclear industry. Cambridge argued that their reports on these surveys should remain confidential because they contain the firm's private recommendations to the client. I accepted the validity of this concern and suggested instead a release of the two studies' complete questionnaires with the marginal results. This request was also denied although Cambridge made a partial disclosure by preparing a memo on that portion of the survey's findings which they felt was pertinent to the issue at hand. They gave the memo to the American Nuclear Energy Council and the Council released it to me.[17]

While not fully satisfactory for the reasons cited above, the partial release (Cambridge Reports, 1979) was very helpful. It contained previously unreleased data from the two proprietary surveys which confirmed the ad's inaccuracies as noted above. It also provided sufficient evidence to convince me that the ad's argument about the public opposition to a nuclear moratorium is misleading. Without the full results, however, I have no way of knowing whether or not there might have been other questions in the survey which would have shown that this generalization about the moratorium was not only misleading but was also in error.

Appendix

Index to Polls on Nuclear Power
Conducted after the Accident
At Three Mile Island

Immediate Post-Three Mile Island Polls

WP 1	Washington Post: April 3-6, 1979 (local, telephone) n=934
HARRIS 1	ABC/Harris: April 4-5, 1979 (national, telephone) n=600
CBS 1	CBS/NYTimes: April 5-7, 1979 (national, telephone) n=1,158
HARRIS 2	ABC/Harris: April 6-9, 1979 (national, telephone) n=1,200
HARRIS 3	ABC/Harris: April 6-14, 1979 (national, telephone) n=1,510
GALLUP 1	Gallup: April 6-9, 1979 (national, personal interview) n=1,322
CAMB	Cambridge Reports: April 7-10, 1979 (national, telephone) n=800
YANK 1	Yankelovich, Skelly & White: early April, 1979 (national, telephone) n=1,024

Later Polls

ROPER 1	Roper: April 28-May 5, 1979 (personal interview) n=2,007
NBC 1	NBC/AP: April 30-May 1, 1979 (telephone) n=1,600
WP 2	Washington Post: May 3-17, 1979 (telephone) n=1,808
HARRIS 4	ABC/Harris: May 18-22, 1979 (telephone) n=1,498

| CBS 2 | CBS/NYTimes: June 3-6, 1979 (telephone) n=1,422 |
| GALLUP 2 | Gallup for Newsweek: July 18-19, 1979 (telephone) n=539 |

State and Local

MA 1&2	Massachusetts/Clark University Public Affairs Center: Feb. 22-March 2, April 4-8, May 1-9, 1979 (telephone) n=1,000
NJ	New Jersey/Eagleton Institute of Politics: April 2-13, 1979 (telephone) n=1,004
NH	New Hampshire/Research Analysis, Inc.: April 27-May 3, 1979 (telephone) n=2,500
WISC	Wisconsin/Wisconsin Survey Research Laboratory: May 15-30, 1979 (telephone) n=650
FIELD 1&2	California/Field Institute: May 3-15, August 3-15, 1979 (telephone) n=ca. 1,000 for each poll
ROCKY	Arizona, Colorado, Idaho, Montana, Nevada, New Mexico, Utah, and Wyoming/ Rocky Mountain Poll: ca. April 5-10, 1979 (telephone) n= 1,016
IOWA	Iowa/Des Moines Register: April 25-28, 1979 (telephone) n=500

Notes

1. I recently prepared a synthesis of the post-TMI polls on public attitudes about the accident and nuclear power in general for the President's Commission on the Accident at Three Mile Island (Mitchell, 1979a). In preparation for this task and as part of my ongoing study of the ethical and value implications of the nuclear debate, I made the compilation of all of the publicly available post-TMI polls

which is the basis for this evaluation (Mitchell, 1979b). I am grateful to the various polling organizations who generously shared their data with me. The Harris organization deserves special mention for their willingness to send the complete demographic breakdowns for individual questions to researchers like myself who request them. Cambridge Reports shared the data on nuclear power from the post-TMI issue of *Cambridge Reports.* Since Roper Reports is available solely by subscription, the only post-TMI Roper Reports data I had access to were contained in the *Roper Reports News Release,* "Early Selected Results: 79-5."

2. Harris has done considerable polling on nuclear power over the years. The two Harris reports for the Ebasco Corporation (1975, 1976) comprise the most extensive analysis of public opinion on the issue which has been publicly available. Although Harris conducted six surveys with questions on nuclear power from April 4 to June 17. Mark Schulman, a Harris vice president, published an analysis of the public's response to TMI based on the Harris polling experience in the August/September issue of *Public Opinion* (1979).

3. The question asked: "Do you think most of the press greatly exaggerated the danger that existed at Three Mile Island, or presented the danger as it really was, or covered up and concealed how dangerous it really was?" By the time of this poll (April 28-May 5) there were conflicting reports about just how serious the hydrogen bubble had been after all. It would be perfectly reasonable for someone to say that the press exaggerated the danger—since the person may have come to understand that the danger was never really there—and also believe that the press did the best that they could do given the information that was available to them at the time. It would have been better to word the question like this: "Given the information that was available to them at the time do you think most of the press. . . ."

4. There is much to be gained by a reassessment of the public's response to TMI at six months after its occurrence, when the President's Commission had made its report and the issue was again in the public eye. My fear, which events may prove to be unfounded, is that while pollsters are good at measuring the immediate reaction to events such as TMI because such events are highly newsworthy, they are not very good at measuring the longer term reaction to specific events once they are out of the headlines.

5. In its weak form the argument is that while public opinion on nuclear power is directly influenced by relevant dramatic public events (such as the resignation of the engineers and the accident at Three Mile Island), these events may also affect longer term trends as well. The strong form of the argument would hold that public opinion simply fluctuates according to immediate events. If one held the strong form, one would argue that the drop in support for nuclear power following Three Mile Island is just another example of the roller coaster in action and that the level of support will go back up when other events, favorable to nuclear power, occur. The trend in Figure 1 does show a decline in the level of opposition in the months following the accident, but as of January 1980 the August level of oppostion was the lowest recorded by Harris after the accident. This level of oppostion represents a small but significant increase from the level which prevailed preceding the accident.

6. The comprehensive Battelle study of public opinion on nuclear power presented the Harris trend with only the 63 percent (1975) and 61 percent (1976) data points. (Melber, et. al., 1977:27).

7. The latest Harris release of this kind is a major study which they conducted in 1978 for a consortium of clients in the nuclear power industry. This study brings the two earlier studies for Ebasco up to date. (Harris, 1978).

8. Consider the difference between two hypothetical distributions of opinion on the seven-point scale. Distribution B shows far more support than distribution A and yet on the existing three-point scale, A and B would show no difference.

POLLING ON THE ISSUES

Should we build more nuclear power plants?

	(A)		(B)	
Strongly favor	3%		15%	
Favor	20%	53%	30%	53%
Lean towards favoring	30%		8%	
Uncertain		14%		14%
Lean towards opposing	3%		12%	
Oppose	10%	33%	5%	33%
Strongly oppose	20%		16%	

9. Harris repeated four questions which were used in earlier surveys. The general wording was: "Do you think _____ is a major problem connected with nuclear power plants, a minor problem, or hardly a problem at all?" One item, "The chance of an explosion in case of an accident" might be taken by the respondent to refer to a) an atom bomb-like explosion, b) a meitdown explosion caused by interaction between the molten materials and ground water, or c) a hydrogen bubble type explosion. Another, "the escape of radioactivity into the atmosphere" is equally vague, as it could refer alternatively to low-level emissions which occur in the course of normal plant operations, to the results of minor mishaps, or to release that might occur as part of a meltdown.

10. The ORC question replicated one which I used in an August 1978 national telephone survey. "In the past several years the anti-nuclear movement has been very active. Do you think of yourself as an active participant in the anti-nuclear movement, sympathetic towards the movement but not active, neutral, or unsympathetic towards the anti-nuclear movement?" The ORC results have not been made public at this writing, but in 1978, 2% were active, 27% were sympathetic, 44% were neutral, and 21% were unsympathetic (Mitchell, 1979c).

11. My preferred wording for such a question is:

At the present time the United States has 70 nuclear power plants in operation plus 91 more plants which are currently under construction. I am going to read you three statements about the use of nuclear power in the United States. With which do you most agree or haven't you made up your mind yet?

    1. We should continue to build more nuclear power plants as needed.
    2. No more new plants should be planned but we should continue to use the ones already in operation and finish those now under construction.
    3. We should stop building nuclear plants including those under construction and shut down the existing ones as soon as possible.
    4. I haven't made up my mind yet.
    5. NO ANSWER

12. Sixty-two percent in this poll favored building more nuclear power plants.

13. A CBS/New York Times national telephone poll, April 5-7, 1979.

14. This proposed amendment to the Nuclear Regulatory Commission Authorization Act would have prohibited the Nuclear Regulatory Commission from issuing construction permits for new nuclear plants until April 1, 1980. It subsequently was defeated 254-135.

15. A Gallup national personal interview poll on April 6-9 found 66 percent rejected the idea that nuclear power plants operating today are safe enough but felt that "their operations should be cut back until more strict regulations can be put into practice." An NBC national telephone poll of April 30 to May 1, 1979, asked people if they agreed or disagreed with the statement "No more nuclear power plants should be built in this country until questions about safety are resolved, even though some say this will mean energy shortages within 10 years." In a previous poll (September 1978) NBC had found 52 percent in agreement with this statement. In the post-Three Mile Island poll this group had increased to 65 percent.

16. This is a quote from the monition preceding a confidential report which Cambridge Reports conducted for a corporation on another subject. This report was subsequently cleared for release to the public by the corporation and is a valuable source of information for the debate over what risks are acceptable.

17. The use of polls in issue advertising has been with us for some time and a tradition of accountability on the part of the polling organizations has generally developed. According to Leo Bogart, the Opinion Research Corporation "repudiated" the use made of some of their data by the "Citizens Committee for Peace with Security" which took out an ad on June 13, 1969, at the height of the Senate debate over the Safeguard ABM system, to proclaim that "84% of All Americans Support an ABM System" (Bogart, 1972:10-12). In this case the wording of the questions was such that it was extraordinary that *anyone* would have voiced an anti-ABM opinion in response to them.

References

Barber, James David. 1979. "Not The New York Times: What Network News Should Be" *Washington Monthly* Vol. 11, No. 7, September, pp. 14-21.

Bogart, Leo. 1972. *Silent Politics and the Awareness of Public Opinion* (New York, Wiley-Interscience).

Cambridge Reports, Inc. 1979. Memo to Mr. John T. Conway, American Nuclear Energy Council, re: Background Data on December 4, *Washington Post* advertisement, December 19.

Ebasco Services, Inc. 1975. *A Survey of Public and Leadership Attitudes Toward Nuclear Power Development in the United States*. Conducted by Louis Harris and Associates, Inc. August.(Available from Ebasco Services, Inc. 2 Rector Street, New York, New York 10006).

Ebasco Services, Inc. 1976. *A Survey of Public and Leadership Attitudes Toward Nuclear Power Development in the United States*. Conducted by Louis Harris and Associates, Inc. November (Available from Ebasco Services, Inc.).

Fallows, James. 1979. "The President and the Press" *The Washington Monthly* October, pp. 9-17.

Gans, Herbert J. 1979. *Deciding What's News: A Study of CBS Evening News, NBC Nightly News, Newsweek, and Time* (New York, Pantheon Books).

Harris, Louis & Associates. 1978. "Public and Leadership Attitudes Toward Nuclear Power Development in the United States," Study No. P2845, December.

Melber, Barbara D. et. al. 1977. "Nuclear Power and the Public: Analysis of Collected Survey Research" (Seattle, Battelle Memorial Institute) November".

Michak, Don and Joseph Bowring. 1979. "Never Say Die: The Nuclear Industry Battles Political Fallout" *WIN Magazine*, May 10, pp. 4-8.

Mitchell, Robert Cameron. 1979a. "Public Opinion About Nuclear Power and the Accident at Three Mile Island" (Washington, D.C., Research Memorandum prepared for the Social Science Research Council for the President's Commission on the Accident at Three Mile Island, available from Resources for the Future, 1755 Massachusetts Ave., N.W., Washington, D.C. 20036).

Mitchell, Robert Cameron. 1979b. "The Public Response to Three Mile Island: A Compilation of Public Opinion Data About Nuclear Energy" (Washington, D.C., Resources for the Future Discussion Paper D-58).

Mitchell, Robert Cameron. 1979c. "Silent Spring, Solid Majorities" *Public Opinion,* August/September, pp. 16-20, 55.

Schulman, Mark A. 1979a. "The Impact of Three Mile Island" *Public Opinion* Vol. 2, No. 3, June/July, pp. 7-9.

Schulman, Mark A. 1979b. personal communication.

Weinberg, Alvin M. 1979. "Can We Fix Nuclear Energy?" *SIPIscope* Vol. 7, Nos. 2-3, March/June, pp. 2-6.

Whittle, Charles E. 1979. *Economic and Environmental Impacts of a U.S. Nuclear Moratorium, 1985-2000* (Cambridge, MIT Press).

Yergin, Daniel and Robert Stobaugh, eds. 1979. *Energy Future: Report of the Energy Project at the Harvard Business School* (New York, Random House).

William J. Lanouette

Polls and Pols —
With a Grain of SALT

PUBLIC OPINION about SALT II has been inconclusive—
but not entirely irrelevant.

Whether or not the Senate approves the new Strategic
Arms Limitation Treaty with the Soviet Union may be one
of the most important foreign policy questions of this cen-
tury. The struggle over SALT II has been compared with the
campaign in 1919 for Senate approval of the Treaty of
Versailles (that ended World War I and created a new world
order in a League of Nations). Some senators, including
Frank Church (D-Idaho), the chairman of the Foreign
Relations Committee, have publicly drawn such a comparison. Although the two documents and two events are
very different, at least their historical importance is
comparable.

Public opinion polling didn't exist in 1919, so we cannot
know how closely the Versailles Treaty foes expressed the
prevailing popular sentiment. With SALT II, however, the
treaty has been negotiated, debated, and considered by the
Senate in a world where news and public affairs are often
shaped by polls and pollsters.

And yet, while the pollsters may be around in great
numbers today, actively pursuing their craft on this issue of
critical importance, the significance and ultimate effect of
their work may prove to be incidental. A review of several
polls about SALT II conducted in the past year[1] reveals
widely varying quality (as measured by precision of the
questions and subsequent analysis provided), disparate
methods, a generally simplistic coverage by the news media,
and scarcely any reference to them by senators and their
staffs.

99

To understand why the polls have not played a more dominant role so far, and why their part in the Senate's decision is unclear, we should consider these questions:

What was the quality, relevance, and timeliness of polls about SALT II?

How were they reported by the news media?

How did they reach—and perhaps influence—the senators who must make up their minds about the treaty?

Even the pollsters aren't sure what's happening; nor are the pundits and politicians for whom SALT II has become a consuming interest. As Burns Roper complained in a mid-July 1979 commentary: "A common expression heard these days is 'the polls show' or 'all the polls show,' as though the polls were uniform in their findings." They are not, he noted, and, "in view of the sharp disparities that polls can and frequently do show, it seems to us dangerous to let sweeping generalizations get abroad as to what public opinion is."

Roper said that "A recent issue of *U.S. News and World Report* stated, 'Opinion polls indicate overwhelming popular support for SALT II—more than 75% according to the latest survey.' While the specific survey is not cited, this may be the NBC/Associated Press poll in February [1979] which showed 81% approving the treaty (down to 68% by April). The last issue of *Roper Reports,* conducted at the end of April, showed 33% favoring passage of the SALT Agreement, with 24% opposing and the balance undecided or having mixed emotions. At no time has *Roper Reports* found more than 42% favoring passage. So, against a *U.S. News* statement that 'opinion polls indicate overwhelming popular support,' *Roper Reports* has never shown a majority in favor of it, and moreover shows favorable sentiment declining."

Roper's complaint isn't just a gripe about a competitor's work, although he did hasten to show how his question on SALT II differed from NBC's. The problem had been raised before, by *Public Opinion* magazine[2] which noted wide discrepancies between the NBC/Associated Press, CBS/

New York Times, and Roper polls on SALT. The differences, the magazine noted, were due in part to differences in the wording of the questions.

At about the same time, these three questions yielded very different results:

1) "Do you favor or oppose agreements between the United States and Russia which limit nuclear weapons?" (NBC/AP, asked 5-6 February 1979) Favor: 81%. Oppose: 14%. Not sure: 5%.

2) "Do you think the United States should or should not negotiate a treaty with the Russians to limit strategic military weapons?" (CBS/NYT, asked 16-17 December 1978) Should have treaty: 63%. Should not: 24%. No opinion: 13%.

3) "The U.S. and Russian negotiators have about reached agreement on a SALT treaty. The treaty, which would last until 1985, limits each country to a maximum of 2,250 long-range nuclear missiles and bombers. As you know, there's a good deal of controversy about this proposed treaty. Do you think the U.S. Senate should vote for this new SALT treaty or against it?" (Roper, asked mid-January 1979) For: 40%. Against: 21%. Mixed feelings: 19%. Don't know: 20%.

As these three polls indicate, the numerical percentages themselves are not "public opinion," but reflections of the public's reaction to certain statements and questions. Roper's complaint about the differences in wording illustrates one of the professional problems inherent in the SALT II data. For no sooner had Roper made his charge than Warren J. Mitofsky, director of the CBS Election and Survey Unit, wrote to him—agreeing with "the general thrust" of the commentary but differing with the analysis. On 18 July 1979 Mitofsky said:

"Your comment about the *Roper Reports* and the NBC/ AP SALT questions is a good example of why one needs to read the introduction to a question along with the question itself. It is my belief that the *Roper Reports* negative findings about the new SALT II treaty are due to one sentence in the introduction, namely: 'As you know, there's a good deal of controversy about this proposed treaty.' I can't help but believe that sentence will induce a more negative reaction from the public, *especially if they don't know already that there is controversy.*

"The NBC/AP SALT question does *not* ask how the Senate should vote. Nor does it ask about the specific treaty President Carter signed. It asks about a principle: Are people in favor of an agreement which would limit nuclear weapons? It has the virtue of not assuming people know the terms of a highly technical agreement, which can hardly be explained in the context of asking a question. It shows that the public supports the principle of an agreement. Additional questions would obviously be needed for a more complete analysis of the public reaction to the actual treaty."

Mitofsky concluded: "I reject the notion that any one of the polls is right or wrong, as you imply in your conclusion. It is more reasonable to believe they are merely different. . . ."

The NBC/AP question that yielded the 81% approval rate last February is now known among pollsters who follow SALT II as "the motherhood question." To answer that question in the negative is to admit, at least by implication, favoring continuation of the nuclear arms race. At about the same time that 81% of those sampled by NBC/AP said they favored limiting nuclear weapons, a poll done for the Committee on the Present Danger by George Fine Research Inc. produced apparently opposite conclusions.

The Fine poll was made between 23 February and 3 March 1979, in response to publicity about "overwhelming" public support for SALT II. It was commissioned by a group that actively opposes the treaty. "Highly generalized, hypothetical and simplistic questions with no effort to measure gradations of response provide data which furnish little insight into relevant public attitudes and are apt to be completely misleading," the Committee noted in its pamphlet.[3] "If you ask the wrong questions, you get the wrong answers."

The first of the Committee's "right" questions produced these answers:

The United States is now negotiating a strategic arms agreement with the Soviet Union in what is known as "SALT TWO." Which *ONE* of the following statements is closest to your opinion on these negotiations:

- I strongly support SALT II — 8.3%
- SALT II is somewhat disappointing, but on balance, I would have to support it — 11.3%
- I would like to see more protection for the United States before I would be ready to support SALT II — 41.7%
- I strongly oppose the SALT II arms agreement with the Russians — 8.6%
- I don't know enough about the SALT II Treaty to have an opinion yet — 29.6%

Based on this question, the Committee drew the conclusion that "71% of those who do have an opinion on SALT II are either opposed to it or want more protection in the treaty for the United States."[4] Even the derivation of this percent is itself specious, for the 71 percent is the result of dividing 50.3 percent (the total of the 41.7 percent wanting more protection and the 8.6 percent strongly opposed) by the 70.4 percent of respondents who said they knew enough to have an opinion. While the conclusion is correct in a mathematical sense, it invites misrepresentation in a political sense.

The Fine poll received wide press coverage, including prominent placement in the *New York Times* and the

Washington Post, and, following the many general statements about the 81% "motherhood" question, it probably left many members of the public thoroughly confused about what their fellow citizens thought. Obviously the public had not shifted dramatically between 5 February and 3 March; the wide discrepancy lies in the polls themselves.*

Beyond Fine's first question lay a host of potentially interesting data in the poll, but this was never analyzed by the general news media. The eighth and final question had the most relevance to the Senate debate that lay ahead, and contained an important political message.

With what you know about the proposed Strategic Arms Agreement, if one of your senators voted against the Treaty, which of the following would be your reaction:

• I would definitely oppose him for reelection	7.9%
• I would be more inclined to oppose him than now	9.7%
• I would be more inclined to support him than now	8.0%
• I would definitely support him	6.1%
• It wouldn't make that much difference; I would make up my mind on his overall record	60.9%
• Don't know/Refused	7.3%

If these data are accurate, then a large majority of the public did not consider their senators' stand on SALT II to be an important election issue. About as many would definitely oppose a senator who voted against SALT II (7.9%) as would definitely support one (6.1%); and those inclined to oppose (9.7%) roughly matched those inclined to support (8.0%) as well.

---

* See New York Times, Sunday, March 18, 1979, "Poll Says Few Back Soviet Arms Treaty" by Richard Burt; and *Washington Post,* March 16, 1979, "New Poll Challenges Surveys on SALT" by Robert G. Kaiser.

This and other polls have shown that the public, understandably, is not strongly inclined to tie the fate of SALT II to its political decisions when it is unsure about both the details and the implications of the treaty.

In the next issue of *Public Opinion* magazine[5] editor David Gergen picked up on the CBS/New York Times finding he reported in his March/May analysis: that only 23% of those interviewed could correctly identify the two countries participating in the SALT negotiations, "and this after seven long years at the bargaining table." Gergen wondered: "If so few people even know who the players are, how can they comment intelligently upon the game, much less the score?"

Gergen then elaborated on problems that pollsters were having with SALT II:

"For survey researchers, that is an old familiar question. Bernard Roshco, former editor of *Public Opinion Quarterly* and now senior public opinion analyst for the State Department, believes that the SALT polls are a classic example of opinion that has not yet crystallized. 'On some issues, of course, the public never has an opinion. But on questions like SALT, opinion often follows a career path. In its early career—and that's where SALT appears to be now—opinion is rough and ill-formed. But when the issue begins to dominate the headlines and evening news, opinion reaches a more mature stage in its career and we can understand it more fully. Opinion on SALT will probably begin to mature when the text is released and the press begins to take a stand.'"

Gergen went on to quote the late Harwood Childs: "... the general public is especially competent, probably more competent than any other group—elitist, expert, or otherwise—to determine the basic ends of public policy. ... On the other hand, the general public is not competent to determine the best means for attaining specific goals, to answer technical questions, to prescribe remedies for

political, social, and economic ills, and to deal with specialized issues far removed from the everyday experience and
understanding of the people in general."[6]

With the passage of time, public opinion about SALT II
did eventually become more focused—probably as a result
of more public attention, as Roshco said is necessary, and
because more information became available, which Childs
noted must also occur. Trend lines did reflect some general
shifts in attitude about the treaty through the summer:
Support fell off a little, opposition rose a little, and the
"don't know" responses diminished. Interestingly, the percentage of those who chose to have "no opinion," as
distinguished from "don't know," remained significantly
large, revealing a hesitation by many people to decide the
treaty's future.[7]

It is difficult to draw many conclusions beyond these,
however, because of many shifts over the past year in the
wording of various SALT II polls. Publicity about the
Carter-Brezhnev summit in June, for example, seemed to do
little to improve the public's knowledge of the treaty itself;
the introduction of exact numbers and terms from the
treaty, after it was signed, did not noticeably improve either
the clarity or the detail of the pollsters' questions. The public
debate that surrounded the treaty continued to focus on
peripheral issues as much as on the document itself.

Politics Without Consensus

Because no clear consensus emerged by the time the
Senate received the treaty from the president, the hearings
held during the summer involved a string of "linkages"
between SALT II and other public concerns. There was no
evidence from the polls about what the public thought to be
the most important elements of the treaty, or about the most
essential conditions for its passage or rejection. The
senators found themselves confronted with a variety of

issues, *all* plausible in public opinion terms since the public had no clear opinion. No arguments seemed too far-fetched in this climate: even the one advanced by SALT critic Paul Nitze (and later proposed as an amendment by Senator Howard H. Baker, Jr., R-Tenn.) that the U.S. assert its *right* to build large missiles even though it has no intention of exercising that right.

The continuing debate over SALT II among the experts shifted quickly from topic to topic—mostly over details too technical to be easily explained in interviews or telephone calls—making the timing of the polls practically meaningless. The polls were timely in dealing with the peripheral issues, however, because these could be more easily stated, and more easily understood by the general public. Thus the public's views on linkage of SALT II with U.S. human rights policies, Soviet adventurism in Africa, and the presence of Soviet troops in Cuba were quickly and clearly expressed.

Pollsters seemed to have a difficult time conceptualizing their questions because, while no issue is further removed from most peoples' lives than the strategic nuclear balance, few are more ominous than the specter of nuclear war. (Indeed, a few arms-control advocates who favor SALT II tried to give their cause a boost by linking in the public's mind the release of radiation at the Three Mile Island nuclear plant with the perils of fallout from even a "limited" nuclear exchange.)

To be sure, linking the very specific and technical details of SALT II with the very general fear of radiation is not easy, as both supporters and critics of the treaty have found. For if supporters could use the fear of nuclear war to assure the public that their annihilation is less likely with SALT II, critics could likewise warn that such a fate is *more* likely with the treaty. And both sides have taken this approach by producing dramatic color films that feature plenty of missiles and mushroom-shaped clouds.

POLLING ON THE ISSUES

Perhaps this sort of linkage—as appealing as it might be to the advocates, pro and con—is part of the reason that the treaty itself has apparently had no clear image among the public, and why the pollsters have had such trouble devising questions that capture the essence of both the SALT process and the fear of nuclear war. As Ronald Steel noted in the *Washington Post* (21 October 1979, pp. Cl-3): "The comic opera imbroglio over the 'discovery' of the Russian soldiers in Cuba has, if nothing else, dramatized the phoniness of the SALT debate.

"The debate is phony in the sense that it is not about the things either its advocates or its opponents claim. Liberals have tried to sell the treaty as a step toward a more peaceful world; conservatives as a device by which the Russians can dominate the world. It is neither.

"SALT II is not about arms reduction and mutual trust, on the one hand, nor about nuclear blackmail and strategic advantage, on the other. Praised for what it cannot achieve and vilified for what it does not attempt, the treaty has been oversold by some and deliberately distorted by others. The general public hardly knows what SALT II is about—and with good reason, for its meaning has become almost entirely symbolic."

While pollsters have an arduous task trying to reduce the details of SALT II to simple questions, they would be equally perplexed if they try to capture and control its symbols. And yet to deal with the treaty in a way that is responsive to public thinking, some attempt to use these symbols seems imperative. Pollsters must proffer suggestions and images in their statements and questions that are simultaneously unambiguous and evocative. And where SALT II is concerned, the task seems impossible.

In 1821 William Hazlitt said the public "knows itself to be a great dunce, and that it has no opinion but upon suggestion." In 1979, I would contend, the public knows itself to be ignorant of SALT's details and implications. Yet the public also knows that it has received insufficient "suggestion"—from its political leaders and its pollsters—to help frame and articulate its concerns.

Borrowing Robert Cameron Mitchell's three criteria for analyzing the function of polls, and applying them to the SALT II situation, it appears that the sampling and reporting of public opinion have failed in two ways to be of much use. In a third way, however, they have made a positive contribution to the policy-making process.

First, Mitchell says that polls can be "event assessors" by capturing the public's reactions to things that are happening. In this role the polls on SALT II failed because of their inability to present complicated and subtle concepts in a simple, usable way: that is, in the form of unambiguous statements and questions.

Second, as "temperature takers" the polls did provide useful evidence of how the public's attitudes changed—and failed to change—over time.

Third, as "issue clarifiers" the polls failed to be useful because they did not explore the ambiguities that underlie the public's hesitation to decide about SALT II. Polls, by and large, also failed to sketch out the broader issues that will underlie each senator's personal decision about the treaty.

In a way, the public has provided pollsters and politicians with some views on SALT that do suggest specific policies. All that needs to be done is to analyze the data already collected. There is, for example, sound support among the public for linking SALT II to an increase in conventional arms spending. The June CBS/New York Times poll demonstrated this, and such a proposal was made by Senator Sam Nunn (D-Georgia) and by former Secretary of State Henry Kissinger in testimony before the Senate's SALT II hearings in July. That idea was picked up by several senators, strengthened by answers elicited from the Joint Chiefs of Staff, and worked through formal and informal channels between Capitol Hill and the White House. It now appears that as a result of this initiative, which apparently has the support of the public, the Carter Administration will submit its defense-budget estimates to the Senate in time for them to be considered in floor debate on the treaty.

A result of the polls? Probably not—or, at least not directly. Yet in this instance, senators considering the connection between their vote for SALT II and a boost in defense spending can cite the public's support for that policy.

About the only senator who has made a direct appeal to the polls when mentioning SALT is Robert Dole (R-Kansas) who said that Republican presidential candidates should be wary of campaigning on an anti-treaty platform because a large majority of the public supports the document. "If the SALT II agreement becomes a partisan issue, Republicans will lose," Dole warned.

Dole made that assertion based on a general question. There is no public evidence that senators are doing the kinds of crosschecking of data that is possible with today's polling techniques. And, even with the CBS/New York Times poll's range of questions in June 1979—the most complete to date—some of the answers elicited were vague. Consider the one on U.S.-Soviet equality. It followed two others on "military strength," so the general terms of reference had been stated. But it made no attempt to differentiate between strategic or tactical, nuclear or non-nuclear, or allied or national forces and weapons.

"If the SALT treaty is approved," the question went, "do you think the United States would then be superior, would be about equal, or would be not as strong as the Soviet Union?" 7% said the U.S. would be "superior"; 42% said it would be "equal"; 27% said it "will not be as strong"; and 23% had "no opinion."

What is a journalist to do with such conclusions? Write a

broad-ranging discourse on the military balance? Try to relate SALT to the stalled Mutual Balanced Force Reduction talks on reducing conventional weapons? Raise the relative importance of economic-versus-military competition in the world?

Furthermore, even when a journalist can work the poll results into a broad piece, the relative importance of the data presents problems. Few journalists are skilled in polling techniques. They are usually rushed in their work. They are urged to simplify and dramatize their material. Only recently have journalists and their editors made a habit of including routinely in their stories the details of how poll data were collected: exact wording of questions, size of sample, date of interviews, etc.

Even when journalists do take the time to analyze polls, their task is not easy. Pollsters, when interviewed, often lapse into elaborate explanations of their methodology. Instead they should try to explain what they considered to be the principal issues, ambiguities, and assumptions behind their questions. With a topic like SALT II, of course, the technical and emotional aspects involved combine to make control over exactly what is being measured difficult for both the pollsters and the journalists—not to mention the politicians on the receiving end of these two producers' output.

No matter what their quality, however, polls will continue to make news. After all, the major news outlets do their own polling with its news value in mind. Once a poll is released, furthermore, the percentage results become the story. Seldom, if ever, do the news media then try to analyze these numerical results, or explain them in terms of other reportage.

In the case of SALT II, as with many other important topics, coverage of public opinion is assumed to be important because elected officials are assumed to care about the wishes of their constituents. But how should this transfer—from perceived public opinion to pragmatic policy—be made? How should the often vague desires of the populace be addressed once their views are collected and widely known? If this transfer is important, then shoddy work by pollsters and journalists alike inevitably poses a serious threat to the responsiveness of our public institutions.

By focusing public attention on the treaty itself, yet failing to explain either its details or its broader implications, many polls have left the impression that opinions are crystallizing. And yet, with a large number of senators still undecided about the treaty and a large percentage of the public having "no opinion" about it, another message also seems apparent.

Consider, for example, the trends that these SALT II polls reveal. Gallup's poll released on 28 October had 24 percent of the respondents favoring SALT II, down from 34 percent in June and 27 percent in March. Those opposing the treaty constituted 26 percent in October, up from 19 percent in June and 9 percent in March. However, respondents with no opinion actually increased slightly: constituting 11 percent in October and June, and 9 percent in March.

Both pollsters and journalists like to find dramatic shifts in public opinion, and the ABC/Harris survey released on 25 October provided just that. The October poll reported a 42 to 37 percent plurality favoring Senate approval of the treaty, and in the ABC/Harris press release announcing these results it was stated that "previously majorities ranging up to 76 percent had approved ratifying SALT II."

This assertion poses some problems. The first question in the October survey was, "Do you favor or oppose the U.S. Senate ratifying the new SALT nuclear arms agreement between the U.S. and Russia?" But the 76 percent figure that ABC/Harris used in their comparison, which comes from a 14 May release, was the result from a different question in a different place on the questionnaire.

In the May survey it was the final question, not the first,

and it followed several specific pro and con statements about SALT II. Furthermore, the May survey asked if respondents favored or opposed "the U.S. and Russia coming to a new SALT arms agreement?" It did *not* ask what people thought the Senate should do if the agreement were ever reached. In that May release, the most comparable general question about reaching agreement (but not about Senate action) showed a 72 to 18 percent approval of SALT.

It is important to note that those "not sure" about SALT II had doubled, from 7 to 14 percent—and this after six months of publicity about the treaty, the summit at which it was signed, and the Soviet troop controversy. This is a trend that commentators missed.

By watching for dramatic swings in public opinion, both the pollsters and the press missed what seems a significant revelation. One question that was identical in the May and October ABC/Harris polls was this: "At a time when it is possible for the U.S. and Russia to blow each other up with nuclear weapons, it is vital for the two countries to reach an agreement to limit nuclear arms." In May, 85 percent agreed with that statement and 12 percent disagreed. Six months later, in October, 86 percent agreed and 11 percent disagreed. In this case the trend line is significant for its *lack* of change, because it reflects attitudes from before the treaty was signed until weeks after the Soviet brigade in Cuba became a contentious issue. And yet, I suspect that because it wasn't dramatic; because there wasn't a change (while for ABC/Harris the 76 to 42 percent shift, however derived, was dramatic), neither the pollster's press release nor the media gave it special attention.

Pollsters should have spent more time trying to define and identify the ambiguities and emotions that surround this document, so that both the public itself and the Senate could have an accurate gauge of the nation's most fundamental priorities. Does the public support the policy of Mutual Assured Destruction, on which SALT II is based? Does the public acknowledge the "essential equivalence" of the two superpowers' strategic arsenals? Does the public believe that the United States *should* maintain a strategic advantage?

Few polls taken in 1979 even attempted to address these basic issues. As a result, the debate is especially ripe for demagogues who choose to provide their own answers to such questions.

Notes

1. For this review I have examined the following polls: For *1978:* Gallup/Newsweek, June; CBS/New York Times, June, November, December; NBC/AP, June, August, October, November, December; the Roper Organization, October/November. For *1979:* NBC/AP, February, May, July, September, October; CBS/New York Times, January, June; ABC, May, June, July, October; Committee on the Present Danger, March; The Roper Organization, October; Gallup, March, April, June, July, October.

2. March/May 1979, p. 27.

3. *Public Attitudes on SALT II: The Results of a Nationwide Scientific Poll of American Opinion* 15 March 1979, Committee on the Present Danger, pp. 4-5.

4. *Ibid.,* p. 9.

5. June/July 1979, p. 60.

6. Quoted in Charles W. Roll, Jr. and Albert H. Cantril, *POLLS: Their Use and Misuse in Politics* (Basic Books, 1972; Seven Locks Press, 1980), p. 144.

7. An NBC trend line from March to October 1979 showed that persons with "no opinion" declined from 79 percent to 44 percent. Those in "favor" of the treaty rose from 13 percent to 25 percent. Those who "oppose" rose from 6 percent to 26 percent. And those who were "not sure" increased from 2 percent to 5 percent. It suggests that those with no opinion will probably remain a large percentage of the public, perhaps even after the treaty is voted up or down by the Senate.

Everett Carll Ladd, Jr.

Looking for the Gestalt:
The Secondary Analysis
of Opinion Data
in Policy Research

DIFFERENT types of questions pose, in public opinion polling, very different situations with regard to the reliability of the information they yield.

Some questions in the polling context are almost certain to provide reasonably reliable information just about every time out. The most obvious instances involve requests for nonsensitive, factual information in areas where respondents have firm knowledge.

"How old are you?" Some people fudge it, to be sure, but they know and they'll usually tell. "How are you going to vote?" If one asks it in mid-October of a presidential election year, one again comes pretty close to capturing reality. Or, "Generally speaking, in politics as of today, do you consider yourself a Democrat, a Republican, an Independent, or what?"—one can be fairly confident that the distributions one obtains are reality.

When one moves into polling on complex policy issues or social questions, things are very different. William Lanouette's very interesting paper makes this observation and documents it nicely with regard to SALT. The point that has been made often enough now, I trust—although perhaps, in a more general context, not often enough—is that there has not been any firm public opinion on the SALT II treaty. There has been no clear set of support-oppose distributions that may be accepted in the way that we can accept the distributions on age, or presidential vote

115

intent in some context near an election, or party identification. Why not? What does one typically encounter in an involved policy area as one tries to do polling?

In the first place, one confronts a lack of information. There is typically insufficient public knowledge of what may be regarded as the "technical side" of these complex questions. (Every important policy matter has at least these two dimensions—a technical side and an underlying value component. On the technical side—and certainly this is the case with regard to SALT—information is often grossly lacking.) Insufficient public understanding of the technical dimension of a policy is especially critical when, as is usually the case with regard to complex issues, the public is truly ambivalent—when it holds to contradictory values in some fashion at the same time. SALT is again a good example of colliding values or orientations in the same issue complex. People want peace, a relaxation of tensions with the Soviet Union, an end to the wasteful and dangerous arms race, a less dangerous world, and so on. But people are highly suspicious of the USSR; doubt that that country can be trusted; fear we're slipping behind the Soviet Union; want sufficient military strength *to guarantee* (not simply *to make likely*) adequate U.S. security; want strength in U.S. foreign policy generally, and so on. If SALT means relaxing tensions and reducing the arms race, yes—people want it. If SALT means taking chances with national security before an untrustworthy opponent—well, people don't want it.

At the technical level or with regard to policy detail, Americans simply have never understood SALT II. At the value level, Americans hold to contradictory expectations and assessments.

This is the kind of ambivalent reaction that one confronts repeatedly in polling on complicated social questions. The question of government spending, the taxpayer revolt, Proposition 13—that area, too, shows extraordinary public ambivalence. Americans want government to do an awful lot, but they dislike many of the things it does and the way it goes about doing them. The contradictory values are held at the same time—and both are real.

This ambivalence should not simply be dismissed as people wanting to have their cake and eat it too. In the face of the complexities of life, ambivalence is frequently the only sensible course. But if one is dealing with public ambivalence about a complex reality, the way one approaches the subject is naturally of extraordinary importance. Different survey approaches—even when each is entirely valid—can produce vastly different results.

In regard to subjects characterized by the technical insufficiencies or lack of information of complex issues and by ambivalence or the presence of contradictions or tensions at the level of values—such matters as (a) question wording, (b) the placement of questions, and (c) the event context of questions—what is happening when the questions are asked—look large indeed.

What then are we to do if we are interested in coming somewhere near truth in the study of public opinion on a complex matter of public policy? My advice is, first, to pay very little attention to individual questions and the responses they generate. One can't believe any single measure—and that's not a commentary on how the question is phrased. One simply cannot phrase *the right question* because there is no one right question in a complex area. Rather, one should look for the larger configuration that appears through many different phrasings of questions on the topic. If a truly pluralistic environment does exist, a good amount of quality polling on a particular subject— looked at in its entirety—will begin to give adequate information.

Using many different survey approaches, it is possible to learn how much technical information the public has. How much technical uncertainty is there? What are the relevant underlying values? Is the public really ambivalent as it approaches some significant aspect of the issue? (I think most professional pollsters know that there is typically as much clarity and persistence at the level of underlying values as there is uncertainty and vacillation at the level of technical details.) One can identify the values, determine how people configure them, ascertain how they come together, and learn what kinds of tensions result in particular instances. How much intensity is there, as relevant values are focused on a specific question in a given context? (Here I mean to point out simply that the *direction* of opinion is a part of the story, and the *strength* with which opinion is held is another.) How much movement or stability does one find in a policy area as one attempts to measure direction and intensity of opinion?

What I want to stress is that opinion on complex issues cannot be determined through single items or a single survey. It can be measured only through a data-extensive mode of inquiry—with many different questions starting from various conceptualizations of a problem.

There are obviously many invalid measures of public opinion on a particular policy issue, but there are also a good many valid measures. Thus, a healthy polling situation is a highly pluralistic one in which after many efforts at good questions it becomes possible through secondary analysis to examine the fruits of these many survey inquiries.

The truth appears—yes, I think one *can* properly talk about *truth* in this context—as, and only as, a kind of Gestalt in a messy data-extensive analysis of many survey items, usually over time. The real question is not whether polling can produce sufficiently firm understanding of public views—because it can—but whether we are willing to pay the price to allow it to do so. I mean pay the price in terms of the amount of survey work it takes; the price in dollars and labor to do the necessary secondary analysis; the price in qualifying and hedging as one begins to move through many often contradictory data. It is not easy. I'm sure our record thus far is not the best. But the tools are available for a very effective survey inquiry into the most involved views on public policy and social issues.

Martin Weinberger

Polls to Sell
Products With

WE AT OXTOBY-SMITH are not pollsters. What *we* do is called consumer or marketing research. Yet there seems to be an evident parallel between what I imagine pollsters do for a living, and what we marketing researchers do for a living.

For example, we are *both* in the business of using interviews as a source of information regarding how *certain* publics feel about certain issues. We are both concerned about sampling, questionnaire design, analytic techniques, and understanding what all of those responses to the questions we have asked tell us about the people we have interviewed.

Since we are not in the business of polling, I will not be saying much about polling. Since there does seem to be a series of significant parallels between what *we* do for a living and what I imagine you do, however, I assume that if I talk about *our* business, some of what I have to say will prove to be relevant to yours.

Let me give you a brief description of Oxtoby-Smith—who we are, and the kinds of work we do.

- For 25 years, Oxtoby-Smith has been in the business of providing information to business to help marketing management make decisions.
- We have worked on a wide range of consumer products from airlines to zippers.
- While most of the work we do focuses on the marketing of consumer products, we also work for banks and airlines and oil companies—companies concerned with public issues.

- Some of the problems we work on may seem distant from the kinds you work on, while others may seem very much in the same territory.

By the way of illustration, let me mention some of the issues we have worked on:

- Why have the sales of wine expanded and how do I make use of that knowledge in selling my brands?
- How do I keep my premium-priced products attractive when consumers are worried about money?
- What are the major resistances to taking cruise vacations?
- Does the public see computers as malevolent and if so, what can we do about it?
- How do you communicate concern for the environment in corporate advertising to a skeptical public?

Let me turn now to the issues I want to present. Essentially, I have limited myself to five observations about the work we do.

First, quite simply, we assume that people are complicated. That means, among other things, that we do our work with the idea in mind that an individual can hold opinions simultaneously which appear to be logically inconsistent and incompatible.

For example, we found in one study that people believe that there is an oil shortage and a need to find alternative sources of fuel; at the same time, they believe that the oil shortage has been contrived by the oil companies.

I'm not talking about different groups of people: one group believing in a crisis and another group skeptical of the oil companies. I'm saying that both sets of opinions were held by the same individuals.

I suppose that the simplest way to explain these contradictory opinions is to note that they are often based on feelings and that feelings don't necessarily follow the rules of logic. If you were to pin these people down and ask them why, if the oil shortage actually has been contrived by the oil companies, we need to find alternative sources of fuel, they would probably hedge and say, "It's partly contrived," or "I'm not really sure how much of it is contrived," or "I'd feel safer if we have the alternative sources, just in case there really is a shortage." That's how people *feel.*

From a practical point of view, the consequences of assuming that people are complicated are critical to the way we work. It means that we don't expect to understand consumer attitudes if we restrict ourselves to examining logically consistent responses to simple questions. We assume that we need a large net and a lot of items. More important, we know that if we don't *look* for the complexity, we won't find it. Our experience tells us that generally, complexity is there, whether we look for it or not. We choose to look for it.

The second notion I want to mention is that we recognize that *people not only have opinions, they have passions.* In our work, if we don't measure the passions, we might be misled by the opinions.

For example, if a manufacturer of toilet paper asked us to find out which of a series of scents he is thinking of impregnating on to the toilet paper is preferred by consumers, we could test the scents and tell him that scent A is preferred over scent B. But we would be remiss in our job if we didn't *also* tell him that most consumers are not concerned about the scent of the toilet paper they use.

Indeed, the only preferences between scent A and scent B that matter are those preferences expressed by people who *care* about the scent of their toilet paper. Those who do care may prefer scent B. (We also have to realize that while people may not care about scented toilet paper *now,* they may come to care when advertising informs them of the wonderful benefits of scented toilet paper.) So when we look at opinions, we make a point of looking at passions. We also try to anticipate passions that are latent, if we can.

Third, we assume the *data are mute.* Data do not speak

for themselves. The assumption that they do is, we think, a serious mistake.

The *meaning* of the data is something that an analyst brings to or derives from the data. Just as an accident described by a half-dozen bystanders may have a half-dozen different descriptions, it seems to us that data are often subject to similar distortions when it comes to interpretation.

Getting to the truth of the accident is dependent on the acuity of the observer. The truth of our data is similarly dependent on the acuity of the observer.

This means we try to understand not only *what* people say but what they *mean* when they say those things. It means we have to be sensitive to the extent to which the wording of the question will encourage a response which is a function of the question, not of the real views of the respondent being questioned. It means that we are alert to the socially acceptable responses. We know that if you ask people if they read a newspaper every day, they say yes. If you ask them if they watch public service programs, they say they do, but ratings don't support the claims.

I would guess that if you asked people if they listened to *The Voice of Firestone,* which stopped broadcasting at least a decade ago, eight percent would say yes. What interests us about that response is that the *claim* to have listened to the program may tell us something about the people who make that claim, even if it doesn't tell us about the actual audience for a non-existent broadcast.

And so, when I say that data are mute, I am saying that findings are not evident, they don't emerge or jump out of the tabular documentation of responses to questions. Findings have to be coaxed, cajoled, and maybe seduced. And if you can't do that well, then you shouldn't be in *our* business.

Some people spend a lot of time and energy worrying about distortions due to sampling or to questionnaire design. We worry about those things too. But we also worry about distortions due to misreading the data.

Fourth, *all opinions are not created equal.* That is, some opinions have greater consequences for actions than others do.

We see it as central to our job to sift through all the attitudes we measure and to identify those particular attitudes which have the greatest consequences to the marketer we are serving.

For example, we did one interesting analysis in which we took all the attitudes toward various brands of orange juice and analyzed the relationship between those attitudes and the volume consumed of the particular brand we were interested in. We were able to identify that set of attitudes which, if they could be modified, would be likely to have the greatest consequences for the volume of the brand we wanted to help sell. If the advertiser has to choose *one* message to deliver about his product, it is our job to tell him which message is most important for selling his product.

The key point is that we see it as part of our job to *differentiate* among attitudes and to use whatever techniques we need to identify those attitudes that are importantly related to brand behavior and to separate them from those attitudes which are not. For us, opinions and attitudes are important only to the degree that they relate to "something else"—that something else usually being marketplace behavior or action. We seek to understand the *consequences* of the attitudes we measure. Measuring the attitudes is a first step, not a final one.

The fifth and final point I want to make is that *thinking is expensive.* I don't know how you budget your work. I do know that a large part of *our* budget is devoted to sifting, analyzing, ruminating and just plain thinking about the attitudes and opinions we measure. Because we assume that people are complex and that data are mute, we also assume that it will take time and money to get to the truth. Getting the data is only part of the job.

It's not easy to get that money. But we make a major effort to persuade our clients that if the study is going to be used to guide a major decision, there had better be time and budget for figuring out what all those responses mean.

Often the actual dollars required for the proper analysis of the data are trivial when compared with the amount spent on the actions that are likely to be taken based on the findings and the financial consequences if these actions are wrong.

Let me summarize:

- *People are complicated*—they often hold contradictory views and we won't know about that if we don't look for it.
- *People not only have opinions, they have passions.* We need to measure both. And we need to look at the opinions of those who have passions.
- *Data are mute*—they do not speak for themselves. The level of acuity of the observer may be a far larger source of error than the sampling variance or poor questionnaire design.
- *Not all opinions are created equal.* Some have more consequences than others. We need to know *which* opinions are potent and which are window dressing.
- *Finally, thinking is expensive.* Part of our work is persuading clients that the money required to get that understanding is money well spent.

These, in brief, are some of the guidelines we use in our opinion and attitude research. I hope they are of some use to those who are called pollsters.

Floor Discussion

ROBERT G. MEADOW*: I think there is one crucial matter related to the questions of polls as "issue clarifiers." We must ask if the polls actually clarify issues, or if pollsters set the agenda and policy context by the way that questions are posed. This is an issue pollsters have to deal with when they consider what they do and what policy-makers do. We have to concern ourselves both with the way in which the policy debate takes place *and* with the way pollsters pose questions and subsequently report their findings to policy-makers.

ALBERT H. CANTRIL: May I exercise the chairman's prerogative to give my own view on that? I think you've hit on something that is terribly important. The question has implications for policy as well as the adequacy of our performance as researchers. Those of us in the polling fraternity tend to operate in one of two kinds of elites: the political-journalistic nexus that drives political discourse in this town or the policy-analytic centers that look for data to fit into various economic models, etc. Each tends to share terms of reference within which public policy questions are perceived. We face the danger, therefore, of having our judgment subsumed in the terms of reference of either of these two elites. The result is that we cast the questions we ask the public within these terms of reference and, lo and behold, we get back statistically reliable measures which may or may not have anything to do with what is going on in the heads and lives of the respondents with whom we have talked.

---

* Assistant Professor of Political Science and Communications, University of California, San Diego.

Issues Into Percentages

CURTIS GANS*: I think there is something heretical in this gathering—at least what I am going to say is heretical. It seems to scream out from Mr. Lanouette's paper and, to some extent, from Mr. Ladd's remarks. That is, I think we know what policy makers ought to know about SALT. I am in favor of more sophisticated polls and more sophisticated questions and more sophisticated analysis; but I am concerned about the degree to which we are making government too representative and too responsive to the polling questions. The outlines of public attitudes as far as SALT is concerned are clearly there. People would like to lessen tension; they don't want to sacrifice American strength. In a series of areas the broad outlines of public policy are there. What is needed in addition, however, is a leadership function that I don't think can be defined by polls. Indeed, we're electing these people to adjudicate these complex and technical questions. This raises a question once we get beyond the level of broad public opinion: To what extent are we remiss if we do not begin to poll the attitudes of elites who may indeed be more important in certain types of more sophisticated decision-making. And secondly, to what extent are we remiss in not reporting the public's lack of information on policy issues?

EVERETT CARLL LADD, JR.: I would just comment briefly that I think Curt's remarks are very important. We focus too much in general on the "yes-no" on SALT or other issues and that may well not be the most important in most cases. In many instances the "yes-no" decision is appropriately a leadership responsibility in terms of executing policy in a highly technical context; people really don't have firm views at the "yes-no" level. What polling can do is clarify the concerns that are most relevant. But focusing so much on the "yes-no" gets us into our greatest difficulties.

---

*Committee for the Study of the American Electorate, Washington, D.C.

WILLIAM J. LANOUETTE: There is a terrible attraction here to numbers. The fact that two-thirds of the Senate has to vote "yes-no" leads to a complicated amendment or reservation process which will allow the issue to be rendered in a "yes-no" form while accommodating all the complexities involved. This is what the Senate goes through. Secondly, in something as important as the future of the US-Soviet relations, there is the appeal of some numerical standard of who is ahead. If it isn't counting missiles and warheads, maybe it is counting the commitment of the public to a policy. In other words, the difficulty about an issue like SALT is that you have a "yes-no" vote at the end of the whole process. Every ambiguity has to be reduced somehow along the way to that ultimate choice.

With specific reference to polls on SALT, it is hard for them to deal with the real policy issues. In trying to analyze the whole SALT debate over the past months, two political issues are involved: the reluctance to face up to what mutual assured destruction is and the unwillingness to admit after thirty years of a nuclear arms race that we are really ratifying an essential equivalence. These issues have never turned up in any of the polls I have seen. How do you explain the subtlety and importance of these two concepts to a person on his doorstep, or over the phone? Yet, unless you somehow do, a lot of the numerical certainty you get in poll results is meaningless.

ROBERT J. CUNNINGHAM: It seems to me that there is a presumption in your paper that the public's opinions regarding the SALT II agreement *should* be instrumental to the SALT II debate. But should public opinion—regarding highly technical issues—be that influential in the final debate? Perhaps public opinion on SALT II should only be used as an indicator of the issue's salience to the American people. Beyond that, each senator is an elected representative to vote his choice for his own constituency.

WILLIAM J. LANOUETTE: In the paper I took to task both the pollsters and the press for their inability to better paint the landscape in which the senators have to make up their own minds. I do think there is a legitimate and important role on SALT for pollsters that has not been developed.

ALTON FRYE*: There is a serious question about what weight opinion data should have on the SALT process, but there is another market-oriented question, namely, what is the market for the leadership function we are talking about? I would like to press Mr. Ladd, particularly, because you have spoken to the ambivalence that is in the data Mr. Lanouette's paper collects for us. We now see some candidates with a strong hard-line tilt in the presidential parade. I think one can say that they are placing bets on the capacity to lead this ambivalent population to a harder line stance. When you refer to the pattern of underlying values, do you have a strong conviction or at least an informed judgment as to whether in this market situation the underlying demand for a negotiated arms restraint with the Soviets is greater than or substantially less than the underlying demand of the population to display suspicion, preparedness, hostility, toward the Soviet Union? Are the bets today that concern in the country from this underlying set of values can be built to a viable, salient body of opinion sound or do you think they are fundamentally in error?

EVERETT CARLL LADD: I have two observations on your interesting question. In this case, and presumably in many cases, it is possible for people to be very much of mixed minds and yet to look to leadership for other than an ambivalent approach. Despite the complexities in the country in terms of values, the public wants leaders to lead. Secondly, Americans don't vote against progress. If an idea

---

* Washington Director, Council on Foreign Relations.

in some fashion is defined as progress, the idea is very hard to put down. My reading is that SALT is in some way seen as progress. And you have to explain yourself pretty carefully if you are going to be against progress in the final analysis.

The Impact of the Polls on the Policy Environment

Of what consequence are public opinion polls in terms of their effect on public policy?

What are the requirements for public opinion polls to contribute, if at all, to better public policy?

As a complement to the perspectives of pollsters and journalists, the third conference panel brings together five individuals who are current or former consumers of polls in various areas of public policy. The panel was a "round table" discussion, relying upon extemporaneous comments rather than prepared presentations. An edited transcript of that discussion follows.

A diversity of experience is incorporated in the discussion: individuals from both Democratic and Republican administrations and from different spheres of policy concern. The Round Table is chaired by Leonard Garment, an adviser to President Richard Nixon until 1973. A glimpse into the White House of Jimmy Carter is provided by his former chief speechwriter, James Fallows. The unique problems faced by a federal regulatory agency are reflected in the comments of Susan B. King, Chair of the Consumer Product Safety Commission. Paul Warnke, former Director of the Arms Control and Disarmament Agency, speaks to the national security community's view of the relevance of polling. And Robert B. Hill, Director of Research for the National Urban League, addresses the adequacy of polls in dealing with issues of concern to minorities.

Reactions to these observations are then offered by two pollsters: Warren J. Mitofsky of CBS News, responsible for a national poll conducted regularly by a news organization within a network, and Patrick Caddell, intimately involved in the current administration's monitoring of public opinion.

AHC

The User's Perspective:
A Round Table on the Impact
of the Polls

LEONARD GARMENT: It required no great sacrifice on my part to leave the practice of law in New York for a day and come to Washington. I suppose that permits a brief observation about the different environments in which we operate, since the basic environment of the law is stability and incremental change whereas the basic environment in which the polling profession operates is one of increasing volatility. So there is, in my own perception of these two environments, a very dramatic contrast.

The volatility of public opinion is due in large part to the immense quantity and velocity of information, data, phenomena, that are introduced into the marketplace of public opinion. In recent years, this has increased—the familiar consequence of the communications revolution. Opinions are increasingly vulnerable. One of the large facts of recent times is the much wider dissemination of information; many people know a little bit about a great number of subjects; and opinions are, therefore, rather loosely held.

This phenomenon in public opinion of milling around of information, arguments, and impressions has produced some of the important political phenomena of recent years, including single-issue and referendum politics, and indeed, the weakening of the idea of representative government. The climate in which ideas are generated and opinions buffeted about is one that makes for increasing volatility. This is the environment in which polls are taken and fed back into what is already an unstable setting, in turn making that setting even shakier.

The members of this panel will explore the impact of

public opinion polling from their viewpoint as users of polling material. The two questions that will be addressed are, first, what are the implications in their own experience of polling regarding the formation of public opinion, and secondly, what if anything can be done to improve—from the public policy standpoint—the relationship between polling and the development of the climate in which policy is shaped.

JAMES FALLOWS: All the reading I've done in the last few days to try and understand what it is you all do has convinced me to be candid about the non-representative nature of this "sample" of opinion. One caveat is that I am the farthest thing from an expert on polls. The only polling data I have seen are those I came across from time to time while working on the Carter campaign and in the White House.

More important, the polling data I usually saw in the government were connected with the *salesmanship* of a program, as opposed to the development of its policy, so I may over-emphasize that stage. One final caveat is that I worked under unusual circumstances, in the following sense: The president I worked for actually believed what many presidents have said, that if it came to a choice between doing what he thought was right (with a capital R) and what people would approve in the polls, he would instantly choose the Right.

Having warned you of the limits, I will proceed to overstate my case. You are all familiar with Ockham's Razor—as a means for analyzing intellectual disputes; I would like to propose "Fallows's Razor" as a way of describing the utility of polls to those making decisions. It is that polling data are useful to the extent that they tell you *how* to do things you have already decided to do for other reasons, and they are potentially damaging and destructive to the extent that they take the place of other ways of deciding *what* you want to do. That is, I found poll data generally far more helpful as a means of designing tactics, of explaining how to get from point A to point B, than as a way to tell you that point B is where you ought to go.

Let me illustrate both the good and the bad sides of this equation. The starkest is an example of a case familiar in politics, especially presidential politics in which the president feels he has a good reason to take a certain action, but knows that most other people disagree. A good example is the Panama Canal Treaty. President Carter felt he had good and sufficient reason to make that decision, but he looked at the polls and found 70, 80, 90 percent of the people thought it was a bad idea. The great service polling data provided was not so much to tell him that everybody was opposed but rather to help explain the reasons for their opposition. The data revealed what people thought the treaties would do and thus indicated what sort of arguments might sway them. With that kind of data—which revealed, for example, that most people thought we owned the Panama territory—you could explain the other side. By showing what things were on their minds, the polls gave the president a better chance to develop effective arguments. A second example which came up early in President Carter's first year was his national energy policy. Once a president decides that he's going to do this or that on energy, his steps toward that goal may be different if he knows that most people don't know that we import any oil. If you have that as a piece of polling data, you can reshape your explanatory campaign—for example, by emphasizing the simple fact of imports.

A third example, from the campaign, was the then governor's proposal to do away with the mortgage tax deduction on the income tax. What Carter *meant* was a general proposal for tax reform, of which mortgage tax deduction would be one part. Eighty percent of the people would be better off with such a step, since most of the benefits of the interest deduction go to the very richest

135

taxpayers. But when it came across to most people as simply getting rid of the mortgage tax deduction that saved them a thousand dollars a year, they were against it; the candidate could not then do what he did with Panama and energy— that is, explain to them what the second and third steps of the reasoning were and why their initial opposition was excessive.

I would like to give two other illustrations of ways in which skillfully used polling data can help sweeten, or put a shine on, something that a politician has already decided to do. It may be that a president decides, for good and sufficient reason, that he needs to spend more money on defense. Once you've made that decision, you will present it differently if you think 70 percent of the people want more defense spending than if you think 10 percent want more defense spending. It doesn't affect your decision, but if affects the sort of rhetoric in which you present it. Similarly, we have the example of the July 15, 1979 speech in which the president talked about the spiritual "malaise" of the country. I know of this only what I read in the newspapers, but my understanding is that polling data—produced by Pat Caddell—freed the president to do what he had long wanted to do, to talk about his basic concerns for the spiritual health of the nation. These strike me as illustrating the beneficial effects of polls—things that were handled more skillfully because of those poll data than they might have been without them.

I would like to give briefer examples of the danger that polling data can cause when they become a surrogate for deciding *what* to do, instead of deciding *how* to do it. Instead of giving specifics, since to give specifics would violate my well-known rule of confidentiality about things I saw in the government, I would like to explain some of the systematic reasons why polling data can mislead you about *what* to do. One of those reasons, as you all know, is that polling tends to emphasize the short-run opinion, the immediate effect, as opposed to the long-run judgment. The clearest example of that is a presidential preference poll conducted a year and a half, two years, three years, before the election. If President Carter had decided to act on the basis of those polls, he would have resigned by now; and one assumes that similar short-term biases are built into polls on other subjects.

Poll data can emphasize the short-run in a subtler but similarly disturbing way. Let me give a hypothetical example: Suppose that an incumbent Democratic president confronted the problem of inflation and knew that he had certain weapons at his disposal in order to fight it. Now he might come across polling data that told him: Look, the people know you can't do anything about inflation, they are resigned to it, they know it's beyond anyone's control. One logical political conclusion might be that he should not do much about inflation, since he'll only get himself into trouble by pretending to do something that no one thinks he can do. That is one of the choices. It seems to me, though, that such a course fails to anticipate that a year or two later the people are going to say, well, it may not be Carter's fault, but we're still going to throw him out because there is 20 percent inflation. In other words, what they say two years before the election about who they're going to blame may not be a good indication of the way they respond when election time arrives.

The third way I think polling data can mislead is that they do not measure the way real political business is done. It may well be true that in a nationwide poll a majority of the people would say that lawyers are bad; doctors are bad; oil companies are bad; banks are bad. You could try to win transitory approval from them by appealing to those prejudices. I speak as someone who has participated in several such appeals. When it comes to enacting legislation to effect many of these changes, however, you work within the very different landscape of the Congress and the various

137

blocs within it. Therefore, polling data showing that 70 percent of the people favor an attack on industry X may tell you nothing at all about the prospects of legislating anything relating to industry X when dealing with the Congress and the real world. Having exceeded my time, I will stop there and let my fellows continue.

SUSAN KING: I speak from the somewhat more limited perspective of a health and safety regulator, one whose experience has been in a specific area of government policy-making. The Consumer Product Safety Commission is a user of polls, not in the sense that we commission them, but rather in that we watch and observe them closely. I know that many governmental agencies do undertake a considerable amount of polling—the health and safety regulators probably less than most because the size of the agencies and the budgets at their disposal do not permit as much as we would like. In addition to being users, we find (particularly in the last two years) that we are often the subject of the poll—and sometimes perceived as the victim of the poll.

The polls that affect us most tend to be from print media, rather than television. They are useful to us in terms of trend analysis over a period of time, the pulse-taking that Mr. Mitchell mentions in his paper. And probably their greatest utility for us as we attempt to analyse trends, at least in the recent anti-regulatory mood, is that polls help us in preparing defenses. They alert us to issues that bother people, for example, problems or ideas or concepts that we are not explaining well and that need more attention. Polls identify issues that we are going to have to deal with. They are good "alerters" in that sense. The polls suggest *how* we should pursue a given objective and, in a negative sense, how we should *not* attempt to pursue a given objective.

Polls are not useful to us (at least from my position) in terms of offering much in the way of policy guidance. That is, they do not tell regulators *what* it is we should be doing, because we operate under rather well defined statutes. What we are to do is quite clear: It's set down in the law.

Another problem touched on earlier is the internal contradictions that we find in polls on subjects we deal with. Contradictions occur because these are very complicated issues. For example, whereas there may be strong registration of public feeling about government regulation in general—a broad majority of the public is opposed to additional government regulation, thinks there is too much government presence in the private sector—when you ask specific questions, almost all the polls reflect a sizable majority in favor of health and safety regulation, particularly in the areas of air and water quality, workplace safety, and consumer product safety. These questions always elicit around 74, 75, 76 percent positive response.

As an example of the contradictions, take a Harris poll in May of 1978, at the time the Consumer Protection Agency was under consideration. Fifty-eight percent of the respondents indicated that they were in favor of the creation of such an agency and 28 percent opposed it. Sixty-nine percent said that creation of such an agency was long overdue, and about 65 percent agreed that the consumer couldn't fight big business alone and needed a government agency to help protect consumer interests. At the same time, 52 percent said that they agreed with the statement that another bureaucracy would just lead to more red tape and higher taxes, and probably wouldn't help protect the consumer at all.

So in addition to what I believe to be a need for more specific questions and more in-depth presentations of issues to people, we still find internal contradictions in poll results when a given issue is pursued within a rather narrow framework. In the Harris poll just referred to, two-thirds of the people were saying that they thought that government assistance and the Consumer Protection Agency were necessary; but half were saying at the same time they thought the agency was doomed to failure before it even started. It's advice to us like that of Alice's Red Queen—do six impossible things before breakfast!

One of the problems that regulators have encountered has to do with the question of whether or not the polls have become a force that drives rather than reflects public opinion. In our experience, they have on occasion. An event in the regulatory community—the appearance of Dr. Murray Weidenbaum's study from Washington University in St. Louis on cost-benefit analysis and how much government regulation was costing the American public—was picked up by pollsters. There followed a shift in public opinion, as Harris reflected a few months later. For the first time, the public registered strong opposition to additional government regulation and, for the first time, agreed with the statement that there is too much government regulation of the private sector. That's a matter that begins to concern us enormously.

The issue of regulatory reform is very complicated. The question of government regulation of the private sector is itself multifaceted and not easily dealt with. I suggest that here polls helped shape the debate. General concern on the part of the public can be specifically focused. In this case, a generalized concern in the population came to be directed rather narrowly at government regulation, ignoring a whole range of other factors that may have had a good bit to do— more than was recognized at the time—with what was bothering people. Here, critics of health and safety legislation and health and safety regulation could specifically interpret a non-specific conclusion. The anti-regulatory theme also was seized very rapidly by members of Congress and candidates for public office. It tends to draw a fairly strong response from the public.

There has been a cyclical effect—poll results fueled political polemics—with the issue growing larger and larger without any light being shed on the subject. What would be more useful to the public policy maker is, obviously, much greater exploration of the issues in their complexity rather than dealing with a very complicated issue in a simplistic fashion. It would also help to have some understanding of the strength of the opinion registered by the respondents, an idea as to the depth of knowledge of the respondents and an indication of why they are responding as they do. Are opinions driven by specific experiences that people have had, or something they read, or newspaper and television coverage of a given issue?

From a regulator's viewpoint, the single greatest problem with polls is that when a question is put to the public very seldom is there a realistic and reasonable alternative posed. We need to ask, if you think there is too much regulation, what programs are you willing to give up? Are you willing to accept what might be the fallout of that? The cost-benefit question that regulators are dealing with right now raises all of those issues. If regulation of carcinogens or if the Delaney clause were no longer applied by the Food and Drug Administration, what health and safety trade-offs are involved?* If you want to get rid of something, are you willing to accept—or at least consider—the consequences? I think that the results here might be quite informative. One of the most interesting polls that I have seen had to do, again, with the question of government regulation. The results were full of internal contradictions—but one of the most revealing was that when asked, "Do you want the government to inform you of a possible product or environmental hazard even though it may not turn out in the long run to be hazardous?" over 60 percent answered "yes."

Perhaps the most fruitful thing regulators can do, to find out if polling is useful to us in public policy-making, is to do the polling ourselves. By working with professional

---

* The Delaney clause (of the Food, Drug and Cosmetic Act) requires that if a food additive causes cancer in animals or humans it is automatically banned.

pollsters to develop questionnaires that fully explore an issue, offer alternatives, and allow people to say they don't really care about government regulation, pro or con—they don't care whether we have square toilet seats or round toilet seats—we could try to answer for ourselves some of the questions that the polls commissioned by others raise and don't answer for us.

PAUL C. WARNKE: Well, I suppose I speak from the perspective of a former user who hasn't quite kicked the habit yet. In government, I dealt with two fairly controversial issues—the Vietnam War and SALT. In retrospect, the Vietnam War was simple. I am not sure what effect polls had on either the conduct of the Vietnam War or our getting out of it; I suspect that perhaps the key was the polls indicating that young people didn't like the draft. And if you eliminated the draft, they didn't care that much about the war.

On SALT, with respect to its effect on substance, I think it is pretty clear that polls can't affect the substance. They are not responsible for the genesis of the talks back in 1969, and you can't conduct a negotiation by referendum. It's hard enough, as a negotiator, to conduct it with the restraints put on you by the Washington bureaucracy. And if you try to deal with polls too, I think you'd get no place at all.

So really, the effect of polls on SALT has to do more with the tactics of the presentation of the case for SALT than it ever could with the substance of SALT. For example, what the polls have shown is that people, obviously, are against nuclear war and would like to see a reduction of nuclear weapons. At the same time, the polls show that people don't trust the Russians. Neither attitude is a judgment on SALT. Rather, the SALT judgment is a combination of these two somewhat conflicting sentiments on the part of the American public. I think this is demonstrated in the poll commissioned by the Committee on the Present Danger, referred to in Mr. Lanouette's case study. To me, the key question there is the question that says, "Check which one of these statements is the closest to your opinion" and provides as one of the statements, "I would like to see more protection for the United States before I would be ready to support SALT II." Now clearly what that says is that you need protection from the Russians and the negotiators haven't given you protection enough. That statement is really telling the respondents that in checking any of the other answers they will be voting against their own safety. Anybody would like more protection if they distrust the Russians, even though they would like to see a reduction of nuclear weapons. So it is a combination of these two factors that, it seems to me, is reflected in the polls and has to be taken into consideration by those trying to present the case for SALT.

Another problem, obviously, is that any time the Russians behave in the fashion we have come to expect which tends to buttress the judgment that they can't be trusted, support for SALT goes down. For example, the revelations about the presence of Soviet troops in Cuba had an immediate and really very prejudicial effect on popular receptivity to SALT.

I have found that the polls have been useful to me in basically two respects. First, I was able to use them occasionally in my negotiations with Deputy Foreign Minister Semenov, the head of the Soviet negotiating team, particularly with regard to verification measures. He would always take the position we were asking for too much in the way of verification, and I would continually point out that, as indicated by the polls and not necessarily reflecting my own feeling, there still was wide distrust within the American public; therefore, verification and their acceptance of our verification position was a *sine qua non* to getting a SALT treaty approved. Secondly, I think I have been able to use the polls in developing presentations to the American public, because based largely on these findings, it has seemed to me that we had to make two points. First, if you are against nuclear war, if you are in favor of the reduction of nuclear weapons, then obviously you want to see the respects in which this SALT treaty does, in fact, lessen the risk of nuclear devastation. Second, you have to recognize that it does not depend on trust of the Soviet Union. If we are able to establish those two points, obviously we are home free. Now in terms of how the polls could be improved to elicit more specific answers, I don't think it is really possible to get much guidance by asking more specific questions. I don't think it would help, for example, to pose questions aimed at finding out how people feel about telemetry encryption; or the distinction between MIRVs, MRVs, and MARVs; or whether functionally related observable differences provide a sufficient basis for distinguishing between those bombers to be counted and those bombers not to be counted. All that the polls can show us at this point is whether, in fact, the message is getting through—whether people are beginning to realize that they don't have to choose between trusting the Russians and opposing nuclear weapons.

ROBERT B. HILL: If you ask what impact polls have had on the organization I represent, or other civil rights organizations, I would say not much—for several reasons. One is a general distrust still in the black community about research in general and particularly research that's done without the involvement of minority persons. The polls have for the most part restricted themselves to the polling of *attitudes* and what we are most concerned about is the *behavior* of people. This is most clear with respect to the polling of racial attitudes. We find increasingly that polls indicate a decline in the attitudes people express in terms of prejudices. In many cases at least the beliefs, the stereotypes, have declined. But somehow this is not congruent with some of the behavioral manifestations of discrimination, especially in housing and employment. So the kinds of research results that have had greater impact have been those that deal also with the behavioral aspects of society's response to minorities.

I also think there is a need to change the formulation of some of these issues. In polling on busing, pollsters found opposition to busing among whites, but also showed that the black community was split on the issue. It wasn't until later, however, that there was any information on how many kids were getting bused. We found that, over-whelmingly, white kids were bused, and that most of the busing was not for any racial purposes. Thus, someone's saying they are against busing has to be qualified as to the type of busing they are against, since most of our kids are being bused anyway. This nuance has been lost in many polls by not really assessing both attitudinal preferences and behavorial realities. I think that there is a real need to attempt to combine these two.

In terms of the interpretation of the polling data, another area I am concerned about is the focus on leadership. A lot of polls dealing with leadership lend themselves to facile interpretations. Take, for example, the question, "Are you for Dr. King or Malcolm X?" Most polls do not permit people to say they are for both men. The results [tend to] produce a ranking based on name recognition alone. The impact of the philosophy of Malcolm X or Dr. King could not be gauged from the results of such polls. Of course, the leadership polls assume that there is one leader out there for black people—an assumption I think that is not warranted. Also, from the black community's point of view, the performance of groups is more central than the impact of individual leaders. Thus, I think there needs to be increased sensitivity to the way in which we interpret some of these data as they relate to minorities.

One of the basic weaknesses, obviously, when we talk about polling which includes minority groups, is that we *are* a minority, a *numerical* minority within any national sample. By definition, therefore, many of these poll results are not as useful to us because we can't find out which subgroups of blacks—those who have school-age children, those who live in certain areas—are against busing. The sample size is too small.

What is called for now is a greater effort to make the data that have been accumulated accessible to many minority groups. I think the information is extremely rich. I'm especially pleased to see efforts, for example, at The Roper Center to increase the accessibility of survey data to some new consumers, particularly minority, policy-oriented, advocacy groups. Because some of the data needs I feel are important are difficult to meet in one survey, aggregating surveys over time holds promise. I'm talking about building up the sample size, to look at certain questions that have been asked over time. A growing number of organizations which are not academically related, are doing research, and are increasingly sensitive to the importance of polling for attitudes and experiences in the black community as well as the Hispanic community. For example, the National Urban League is now conducting a national repesentative sample of the black population (close to 5,000 black families). It will be one of the largest needs-assessment surveys of blacks conducted across this country—in rural areas, central cities, and the suburbs. We are particularly fortunate in that we were able to retain the services of Mathematica Policy Research and notably those of Irving Crespi, in helping us design our sampling frame and get support from many other sampling experts.

I think this is a harbinger of things to come. We anticipate that there are many types of users, consumers, and organizations with staff persons who have been well trained in survey techniques and analysis. We really have to be aware that there are other users of polling data and that, as a result, some of the interpretations, some of the conventional wisdom, will inevitably be challenged. This will contribute to new priorities and new issues for research. In the area of data collection, there is going to be a call for more quality data about minority groups—this will mean linking up with community-based organizations. I think it is almost inevitable.

We think the movement toward the increased use of telephone interviews is somewhat unfortunate in that it creates a bias, particularly regarding minorities, who are less likely to have telephones. We are going to have to rely more on the kind of linkage that comes through partnership with community-based groups that can gain access in the community. That way we could at least be certain that the kind of information we are getting indeed does reflect a reality—not some illusions pre-ordained by our methodology.

LEONARD GARMENT: Before calling on our two commentators, I will ask the members of the panel whether they have some comment they would like to make with respect to what has been said to this point.

JAMES FALLOWS: I would like to comment on something Susan King said, which may enable me to explain more clearly what I was trying to explain at the start. She mentioned polls about attitudes toward regulation—do the people want more, do they want less, how do they like it? I think that kind of poll can be very valuable in one sense. If you have a certain outlook toward regulation as an elected government official, those polls can tell you how you can best explain your policy to the public. And, in deference to Pat Caddell, many polls that he provided were helpful in that way—helping us better explain things that the president wanted to do. But it is only a small step to a very large difference in the way you use those data: when you start to say, well, if most people are against this or that policy, we'll change *our* attitude on those policies. We won't try to explain our decision in ways that meet the public's objections, as revealed in the poll, but we will instead act as if the polls are immediate referenda on the goals of our administration.

Now my view on this may be Luddite, but I think that's what the Congress is for, that's what quadrennial elections are for, and that's what the normal vehicles of political accountability are for, and it's *not* what polls, conducted every week or every month, are for. I think you have the danger of a much less stable political system and even less courageous political leadership, if you have that sort of instant referendum on what the policy should be. So I would rather see polls of the sort Susan King mentioned used to alter tactics rather than to alter goals.

SUSAN KING: This is how we've tried to use them—to pinpoint issues that need better explanation or to find a better approach to an issue. In contrast, interest groups [sometimes] use polls [in attempts] to [alter] policy [substance]. Typically, the issue is a complex one, the decision relatively narrow, and the process subtle. It involves taking poll results on broad public sentiments and aiming them at a very specific target, [then] bombarding the regulatory agency with the findings. That's where I get very concerned about polls themselves being the cart before the horse, and becoming the vehicle and the weapon by which interests attack and attempt to influence public policy. It's a very difficult position for the regulator—to try to fight back under what I consider unfair circumstances and without any mechanism with which to fight back on the same ground.

PAUL WARNKE: At the risk of repeating myself, I think that there is a difference between influencing regulatory policy, as it has been described by Susan King, and influencing national security policy. I think national security policy tends, by its very nature, to be elitist. It is only fairly recently that the executive branch has been willing to recognize that perhaps the Congress has a role in it! And as far as bringing in the rest of the public, that's really unthinkable. So it is, I think, a particularly elitist field; and one in which the polls are more apt to be used in policy implementation rather than policy formulation.

JAMES FALLOWS: Could I just add one thing to that? I've noticed the looks of stark incredulity on your faces as I've said it, but I still think it's true: President Carter has so far been abnormally staunch, and sometimes crazy, in his insistence on doing what *he* thinks is right, rather than what he sees in the polls. But perhaps the experience of his first few years will convince him to rely more on this referendum style of deciding upon goals. Every week or two, when he is undertaking one of his plans on energy or foreign policy, there are polls in the paper—do you think this is a good idea, do you think this is a bad idea? With the growth of this instant participatory democracy through the polls as a major part of the political process it becomes an un-stoppable phenomenon, but I don't think it's a good one.

ROBERT HILL: With regard to the utilization by policy makers of public opinion polls, we see it more as a two-step flow process to target those individuals who influence policy makers. We find that policy makers are quite busy and have no time to read research results of polls, so we target those who have an impact on policy makers. Increasingly I think we affect them more that way.

Comments
and Observations

WARREN J. MITOFSKY: I suppose my concern is that complicated issues of public policy are addressed superficially by polls conducted by the media. I see most of the media polls (including the ones we do) as following news events, and in lots of ways the reporting of polls by the media is by definition simplistic. It's just not possible in a short amount of time to devote sufficient attention and analysis to what I see as very complex public issues.

There was some mention—by Jim Fallows and Paul Warnke—of interpretation of issues based only on single-question opinion items. None of these public issues is that simple, and I don't see how you can detect a direction or an understanding or even an interpretation of the public mind with simplistic questioning. I like Susan King's idea about more polls being done by the agencies themselves if they would really like to get at—and understand—complex issues. And while I say that, I have some reservations. A General Accounting Office study that came out a year ago discussed the need for better guidance and controls for improving federal surveys of attitudes and opinions. (A famous and well-read document!)

I see polling as a complex process involving technical methodology like sampling and estimating—those mundane notions that have been passed over blithely. Reseachers claim they can hire statisticians for those things. Well, anybody who says that usually doesn't! I saw this lack of emphasis when we stressed simply question wording in our discussions of policy. I think we need to go well beyond question wording and talk about concept. The pollster, no matter how diligent, no matter how well-read on question wording, really can't get at the subject without some proper understanding of the concepts that need exploring and how they might affect public policy. I am not quite sure that is the role of the media polls.

What is needed is the interpretation *for* the policy maker of what the poll really says and what it doesn't say. I am a little concerned that this analysis is often done by people who are not experienced analysts of survey data. To adequately analyze the survey data, you can't interpret merely from those things we put on television or in the newspapers. You need the raw data; you need to play with it; you need to massage it; you need to get at it more.

I am heartened to see that people pay attention to polls, but I would like to see some discrimination in the way they are used. Does the poll get at the important concepts? Is there proper analysis? I suspect far too often a single item is misleading. Any subject we pursued in detail, the more we learned. I'll offer one example: For years we had pursued the topic of abortion and a woman's right to abortion. The public support for the right of abortion has been over-whelming. We noticed that same overwhelming support disappear when we asked about using federal money to pay for abortion for poor people. This was a contrast to public willingness to put up federal money for all kinds of other programs. They were willing to see it used for contracep-tion, birth control, and other more expensive programs, but not for abortion. As we pursued the subject, more and more trying to understand it, the negatives all started to emerge when abortion became a personal decision as distinct from the rights of others. It took about two years to finally understand what was going on. I don't suggest we were very clever; had we been clever we would have understood it sooner. But, by the same token, regarding other complex issues such as SALT or the regulation of different govern-ment programs, I just don't see quick conclusions from the data now publicly available. And I guess I urge a different approach.

POLLING ON THE ISSUES

LEONARD GARMENT: What would you urge in the way of a different approach? There are notions of accountability that are vaguely talked about in relation to public opinion survey work—and you raised some concerns about the interpretation of polls and the extent to which complex material is oversimplified or reported in a misleading way. What can be done about that?

WARREN J. MITOFSKY: Well, there are several approaches. One is depositing of public poll data in a place where they are available for more careful scrutiny. I think policy makers can avail themselves of that kind of information. They could work with more professional people in the interpretation of material, as the State Department has with the operation that Bernie Roshco runs. Perhaps there should be more professional interpretation of public policy polls—it's too casual at the moment. The information is there, the people are there, and I think it could be a little better directed than the general approach I now see.

LEONARD GARMENT: Do you think it is desirable and feasible to institutionalize that kind of mechanism in the government? Do you think that there is a role for government to play in either an existing or a new agency that would undertake to collect the polling materials and publish what would be authoritative summaries or analyses of the material?

WARREN J. MITOFSKY: I see that in what Bernie Roshco's doing at the State Department, to a limited extent. And I would heartily endorse that approach to the use of public materials for policy makers. But to know whether this would work generally in the White House, or in a consumer agency, or in other places, I suppose it depends on the quality of the institution. I think it's possible, because I think there are people capable of doing this, but it really takes a much more serious effort than what's going on now or what is described in the conclusions of the GAO report. GAO's only solution was to dump another bit of work on an already understaffed Office of Management and Budget. I could endorse the State Department type of effort or the Congressional Research Service type of effort, but I am not sure how they would be carried out at other agencies.

PATRICK CADDELL: I just want to raise a couple of other points in relation to attitudes about public polls and the role they play. First, I always sense the attitude among policy makers, politicians, and the press that polls that agree with what they want to do are very good and polls that disagree are very bad. The second point is about how upset people get by the fact that the public is either complicated or often contradictory in terms of its feelings.

There are three things that concern me about both public and private polls in terms of public policy. One of them is the concept problem Warren just talked about: As we become a society composed of experts in narrower and narrower fields, we look at public opinion only in very narrow areas that we're interested in. If we're interested in economics we're really only interested in how people think about economics. Experts interested in politics or energy or regulation or whatever, take a similar approach; never seeming to attempt to blend or to weave in the fact that all these things are related. People do not think in pigeon holes about different problems; they don't get up and think only about economics separate from energy; and they don't get up and think about SALT as separate from how they feel about the general conditions of foreign policy or even domestic policy.

One of the best examples of this phenomenon—and one I find most distressing—is the field of energy, which is one of our most important problems. Over the last four or five

153

years, either privately, semipublicly, or publicly there have been dozens of surveys conducted and hundreds of questions asked and thousands of people interviewed. The deeper you probe into energy, the more you understand that it cannot be approached independent of other issues. As you dig, begin to do complicated sets of analyses, probe new areas, and follow tangents, you find some very interesting things. People's attitudes in relation to energy have a lot to do with how they feel about the question of growth in our society, an issue which is really only now developing. Although growth is a recent issue, people's feelings about how much growth we should have as a society and what they are willing to trade off for it constitute an important subject.

These concerns seem to have as much impact in determining their attitudes as anything directly related to energy. Also influencing attitudes toward energy is the whole question of how they behave (the behavioral mode) as consumers. Nonetheless, our instinct is always to narrow the focus and I wonder sometimes whether our problem is that we shouldn't broaden it again. We're looking for arguments as opposed to understanding. That broader view seems to me to be the most important and most overlooked use of public opinion surveys in that realm.

That leads us right to the whole question of analysis, because obviously it is very hard to bring things together—to look at the wide areas of attitudes or the broad context—unless one does the more complicated analysis Warren suggested. I suppose that is my biggest problem with public polls—how sparse the analysis is. Partly because people seem to be very anxious to get numbers on some questions, they don't seem to want to give very much time to explaining either in print or on the air. More often, by the way, policy people or political people are not interested in analysis either; they are interested in something they can count quickly and make snap judgments on. It's somewhat our fault, I suppose, that as a profession we don't insist more on analysis, particularly when data alone can be misleading.

Now let me go to the most devastating example in terms of policy or decisions in the public arena: the whole question of Watergate. We now know, if anyone is interested, that from the summer of 1973 to April of 1974, we had a situation (which most of you reporters will remember) in which you would all come to us and ask us how dumb the American people could be. If they believed Richard Nixon was guilty, why did they oppose impeachment? I remember article after article about this, castigating the American people for believing this, the Constitution and so on.

Yet a number of private polls were finding the situation to be this: When you ask people what they thought should be done, if it were *proven* that Richard Nixon had committed a crime, huge numbers from the outset said that he would have to leave office. We found when we quickly analyzed the problem that it was due in part to the word "impeachment," and in part to the way the press treated it. Impeachment was viewed as a summary execution process and not a question of due process of law. In fact, when you asked people whether there should be investigation by the House or a kind of indictment process or a trial by the Senate to determine guilt or innocence with the consequence of leaving office, you got massive switches in the data in terms of people favoring that process.

The public polls didn't catch up with that phenomenon, really, until January, February, March of 1974. And the consequence (one I thought most fascinating coming, as it did, after several hundred years of trying to teach some concept of jurisprudence in this country) was, of course, that the balance of control on those Watergate questions seemed to be held by people who personally believed that Richard Nixon was guilty, but didn't believe you could throw him out of office unless you had some process to prove his guilt. This seems to me an entirely rational kind of process. So the attitude of many people on the Hill and in other segments of the elite was, "As soon as the polls show that the majority of the people are ready to impeach Richard Nixon, that's when we should make a move on him. That's what we should do; we have to wait until it gets there, and then we can do something."

This attitude leads me to my third point, which concerns leadership and followership, exactly the point raised in the memo that was sent out. One of the things that concerns me most is the tendency to substitute what seems to be general public judgment for leadership. The positive aspect of this phenomenon, particularly in terms of foreign policy, is the ease with which public opinion can be changed. If you had gone out and asked people about recognizing Red China in 1971, I doubt that the numbers would have changed significantly from what they had been for years. Yet when President Nixon did it, and explained why we were doing it, the support and reaction were overwhelmingly positive. Examples of this are endless.

When you ask people what we should do about solving specific problems, ask them to make more literal judgments than they are willing to or feel capable of or feel it is their role to make, oftentimes you will get a candid answer: "That's what we elect public officials for." On many issues people don't have strong feelings or opinions, and want leadership on where the nation is going and why. Except with obvious issues about which there is a great deal of information and intense feeling, most people are content to move in the direction our leaders indicate.

I am concerned about the simplicity with which people in the public policy area seem to want to gather data. The kind of data they want usually has a highly specific orientation to their own fields and policy positions. The very narrowness of their interests raises the question of pollsters' taking the initiative with broader analyses, to provide greater understanding of public opinion for those in public life.

LEONARD GARMENT: Now before we turn to the audience for questions, does anybody here want to make further comment or responses to the commentators?

JAMES FALLOWS: Could I ask one brief chicken-and-egg question, mainly to Mr. Mitofsky? I think the people I knew in the White House would share your complaint about the news simplification of the public opinion polls; but then they would see each night on CBS News that "everybody is against SALT, for the Panama Canal Treaty, feels this way or that way." Where does one break this cycle of simpleminded numbers? Why can't your organization do better?

WARREN J. MITOFSKY: Well, that cycle has to be broken in terms of the formation of policy based on the simpleminded information. I think the media are trying to improve their analyses. It is only in the last eight or ten years that news people have had any experience at all with polls, but I see change and improvement. I don't see improvement when policymakers repeat the headline portion of what happened on TV or in the paper. The only thing that seems to get picked up is the headline—and not the analysis. Although news analysis has improved, it still isn't an adequate basis for making policy decisions.

JAMES FALLOWS: Might it be better if the news media didn't put out that simple number at all?

WARREN MITOFSKY: In some cases, probably. If the topic has not been publicly discussed and understood then I think it is not in the public interest to present numbers. If a topic has been before the public and had some discussion, then I would prefer reporting the state of mind of the public based on a poll to a reporter's interpretation of public sentiment. I would rather see an interpretation of the public

157

mood from a poll than from the collective wisdom of journalists.

PAUL WARNKE: I just have one question that I would like to put to Mr. Mitofsky and Mr. Caddell. It is one of the questions that was in the material circulated to the round table participants before this session: Have the polls affected the quality of leadership in this country? And if so, how?

I was thinking back to the 1972 election when Senator Muskie was scoring so high in the polls. When it came to the initial tests of the primaries, however, his support was so far below the predictions in the polls as to functionally knock him out of the race. Something of the opposite phenomenon may have occurred with respect to President Carter. In other words, do the polls have almost a kind of boomerang effect? You are up for election and you're doing well in the polls and all of a sudden you get a test, and the actual test of the voters turns out to be very different from the poll results. Does the poll have the unanticipated effect of building up expectations that won't be satisfied when the same voting results in the absence of the poll might have been regarded as quite a satisfactory showing?

WARREN MITOFSKY: Yes, we were referring to him as President Muskie in those days! I think you are comparing different things. The polls that you are referring to were national polls, talking about a national impression of a candidate; and the campaign was in New Hampshire and other early primary states. . . .

PAUL WARNKE: But the effect was the same, because it did build up the expectation that even on a state-by-state basis Muskie would do very well. Then, when he was running for the first time in his own backyard you would expect, if anything, something better than the national results portrayed by the polls.

WARREN MITOFSKY: I think what happens in a primary state is based on the quality of the campaign in the state and can be way off the results of any national poll.

PAUL WARNKE: I recognize that there can be that distinction, but what I am saying is that were it not for the poll, would the result in New Hampshire, for example, have been regarded as quite a satisfactory performance? As I remember it, he failed to get a total of 50 percent; and based on the previous polls everybody had figured that he was going to score a very substantial majority of the votes.

WARREN MITOFSKY: I think the expectation was based on a lot more than just the poll. It was based on his proximity to his home state and lots of other things. The notion that a relatively unknown national candidate could do reasonably well was more responsible for that expectation than anything else. I don't know whether that leads to poorer candidates or better candidates but I think it frees candidates to some extent from the structure of the political process that we used to know. That may not lead to better candidates, but it changes the system quite a bit.

PATRICK CADDELL: In truth, in the last decade and particularly in presidential politics, there's a problem with the way polls are judged. Misreadings or misunderstandings of situations occur most often because poll findings too often exist in a vacuum. If everyone—the elites, the people with money, the media—take their cues from us pollsters, the expectations for the performance of the front-runners become very hard and very real. Senator Muskie's difficulties in New Hampshire were not a function of just receiving 50% of the vote against McGovern and others in that distinguished field. The more central problem was that he was exposed to a greater degree of scrutiny by the media at a time when his opponents weren't necessarily being held to the same standards of judgment. In a free-choice world, I don't know many strategists in a national situation who would prefer [not] to be in second or third place with a lot of potential rather than being a front-runner—particularly by any sizable margin.

LEONARD GARMENT: Pat, could I ask you a question about the general impression I have of increased volatility of public opinion—an immense range of opinions on a large number of subjects that are all susceptible to rather rapid shifts? I have the feeling that opinions are [generally] value-based in general terms and that, as a consequence, these opinions are not firmly rooted and are subject to manipulation. Does your own experience confirm that sense? And if so, why does it exist?

PATRICK CADDELL: Well, this is a tough question to answer. I think to some extent that your impressions are accurate. The interesting thing is that the opinions people hold most strongly are not their political opinions or their opinions about policy issues but their opinions on individual value kinds of questions like abortion. There is some theoretical understanding of this point.

We do see a greater degree of volatility and willingness to change. We can see vote numbers move rapidly and almost capriciously in the general election as well as the primaries. In places like Illinois in 1978, shifts seemed to occur on an hourly or daily basis. I have looked at the analysis of many attitudes about party and ideology that suggests the erosion of many of the anchors on which people could be sure of their judgments of who they are, what they stand for, and what their expectations are from the system. As the anchors erode, the choice becomes a less important choice. I have always been fascinated by Anthony Downs's economic theory of democracy: the radical notion that people will vote in their self-interest, in the sense that you can quantify their judgments to some extent along lines of economic theory, and that people make marginal judgments based on their expectation of what the outcome will be. As you lower the expectation, the outcomes will be different. That has clearly happened between parties and candidates—certainly to an unprecedented degree in '78. The view is that neither party is able to solve the problems or change the problems, and that most candidates are unable to solve the problems, even though people may believe that they are solvable. It reduces attachment to the vote decision. As a party's perceived ability to deal with an issue subsides as a reason for a vote, one begins to make judgments on other factors that may appear to be less important than the criteria we held as important before. I think that, in part, explains why we are seeing the kind of volatility you are talking about.

Floor
Discussion

LEO P. CRESPI*: Three of our speakers have shown a rare degree of consensus on the thesis that polls should affect policy tactics but not policy goals. I find that a very distressing point of view. When President Carter reaffirmed his commitment to the Jeffersonian injunction to pay a decent respect to the opinions of mankind, he was either suggesting that he was open to potential revision of his goals, or entirely misrepresenting his position. When I survey people in other countries, I am interested in what their goals are; I'm not interested in tactics to impose our goals on them. Goals embody values and people can be surveyed on values better than anything else.

JAMES FALLOWS: Long before the debut of opinion polls, there was a system of representative democracy in which candidates faced the electorate and elected congressmen were accountable to the people every two years.

PAUL WARNKE: I was addressing one particular issue, the Strategic Arms Limitation Talks. I don't think the president of the United States should find out in advance whether the American public favors strategic arms limitation talks. It should be obvious to anybody in the national security field that nuclear war is bad for you and anything that you can do to minimize that chance is in the interest of the American public. Even before the initiation of the talks, you shouldn't find out whether a majority of the American public favors your making that effort. An elected official must take certain matters as his own independent responsibility,

---

* Office of Research, International Communication Agency.

whether popular or not. I would feel quite differently about the Vietnam war, another controversial subject that was very hot when I was in government before. In such a case I feel quite strongly that ascertaining the sentiment of the American public is absolutely essential. You shouldn't conduct a war—as a matter of fact you can't—unless the American public is behind you. You have to look at what the particular issue is to determine whether a poll is going to be useful and perhaps even essential in determining the substance of your position. Even on a matter as cardinal to security as the nuclear arms limitation talks, a decent respect for the opinions of mankind does affect what you do. In August 1968 we were about to announce that the strategic arms talks would begin in September. But that very day the Soviets moved into Czechoslovakia and made it impossible for us to convene talks crucial to our security— and it didn't take a poll.

SUSAN B. KING: Let me interject a comment in a narrower frame than national defense policy or the many issues that face a president. Many other government policy makers find that the utility of poll data is limited to tactical decisions rather than goal-oriented decisions. But, as a regulator, I would like some specific guidance in several areas. Robert Hill talked about attitudes among minorities. Any consumer agency constantly faces questions about attitudes in minority communities. Do the problems differ in communities that are more conscious of health and safety issues, for example? We have talked about polling in the minority community to help set goals and objectives and to establish means to achieve goals articulated by the communities themselves. This is very important. But we find polls to be of limited use in the larger sense of goal-and-objective-setting.

BARRY SUSSMAN: We've all heard of examples of absolute attempts by presidents to use polls to manipulate public opinion. How serious are most attempts to use data, or a sense of where the public stands, to manipulate the public on an issue? Is this something for us to be worried about?

LEONARD GARMENT: I had thought of raising the question at the beginning, at the risk of sounding like a man who has had an active career pressing one point of view that turned out to be wrong. But I continue to feel there is a real danger in the immense amount of polling material now available. It is a fertile area for manipulation, whether intentional, unintentional or both. Government, private institutions, or private individuals involved in a political or advertising campaign can use the precise technology to identify those issues on which people are vulnerable and then to tailor a campaign that sells an idea to the exclusion of all other competing ideas and values. I think there is added danger in this regard because of the pervasive yearning for coherence abroad in the land.

JAMES FALLOWS: Mr. Sussman's question is the first suggestion I've heard in a while that President Carter had been excessively skillful in manipulating his public relations. I agree there is a danger that the politician's natural and healthy desire to stay in office can lead to manipulation, because of the superior tools available. That, in turn, is a mirror of the dangers that every other technology presents.

JIM KARAYN*: Mr. Warnke, do you think the president should use public opinion surveys to determine what to do in Iran?

PAUL WARNKE: My answer is very clear—no! In the first place, it is too late; and in the second place, I don't think you

---

* President and General Manager, WHYY, Philadelphia.

could formulate a question which would give him any useful guidance. This lies preeminently in the province of the commander-in-chief. American lives are immediately in danger and he ought to react in a fashion that he and his advisers feel is best calculated to preserve those lives.

PART IV

Polling:
A Political Institution?

Have the polls become a political institution in their own right and, if so, what are the implications for the future of polling and its relationship to journalism and the policy process?

The presentations of the concluding conference panel deal with three aspects of the overall question about the role of public opinion research in our political process.

George H. Gallup opens the panel. From both an historical and international perspective, he considers the place of polling in a democratic system of government in general, and the balance between majority and minority opinion in particular.

Harry W. O'Neill delineates some of the dilemmas faced when opinion research is conducted for special interests. Specifically, he looks at the place of "advocacy research" in the field of polling and asks how the legitimate right of special interests to commission polls can be balanced against questions about the credibility of all "non-advocacy" opinion research when advocates use poll findings to argue their points of view.

Mervin D. Field closes the panel, examining some philosophical and practical aspects of how and when polling serves and disserves the public interest.

AHC

167

George H. Gallup

Preserving
Majority Rule

PUBLIC OPINION POLLS, based on modern sampling
methods, have been conducted on a continuing basis for 45
years, or approximately one-quarter of the total number of
years that the nation has been governed under its present
constitution.

I believe we can safely conclude, therefore, that polls are
here to stay and the question which we now must ask is how
this instrument fits into the democratic process, and, more
to the point, how polls can improve that process.

A member of the House of Representatives, on the
occasion of his retirement after many years of service in that
body, was asked how much attention he, as a member of
Congress, had paid to poll findings. His answer was, "Very
little."

The reason, he added, was that the views of the numerical
majority, as reported by the polls, fails to take account of
the degree of understanding that the public has of a given
issue, and overlooks the intensity of the feelings of those for
and against.

The views expressed by this congressman are shared, I am
certain, by most members of the House and the Senate—
and especially by those congressmen whose states or
districts can be won or lost by a small shift in the vote at
election time.

The root problem is that a well-organized minority, ready
to cast its votes for or against a candidate because of his
stand on a given issue, ready to knock on doors during an
election campaign, and ready to contribute substantial sums
of money to a campaign, carries far more weight with an
officeholder running for re-election than simple numerical
majorities.

168

If these assumptions are correct, then at least three important conclusions can be drawn. The first is that few, if any, members of Congress are poll-followers as is frequently charged by those critics who see danger in the alleged influence of polls on the legislative process.

The second conclusion is that majority opinion is not necessarily a controlling factor in the legislation that emerges from Congress.

And the third and by far the most important conclusion is that we now seem to have reached a point when well-organized minorities can and do thwart the will of the majority.

A classic example, of course, is the gun lobby. As early as 1938 we found in polling the adults of the nation that 84 percent favored registration of hand guns with the government. And we have found large majorities in favor during the 40 years since that early poll.

Congress has been so bribed with campaign contributions, and intimidated by the National Rifle Association lobby, that no effective legislation has ever been passed. What is even more disturbing, the fantastic success of the NRA has shown all the other pressure and one-issue groups just how to go about dealing with Congress to get the legislation they want.

Examination of legislation and election returns of recent years clearly reveals the growing strength of organized minorities. We must begin, therefore, to do some soul-searching. Are we, as a nation, prepared to give up the democratic ideal of rule by the majority for rule by organized minorities? If we still believe in majority rule then we must begin to give serious thought to ways of preserving it.

Based upon my own experience and observation, I believe there are at least three ways to do this.

The first is to make greater use of the initiative and referendum—both on a state and national scale. The initiative and referendum establish majority opinion of those who vote, and give this majority opinion legal force. Although participation in a referendum (unless it is compulsory) can be disappointingly low on occasion, at least it offers every citizen an opportunity to register his opinion.

And single-issue minorities, despite their most vigorous efforts, would find it difficult to reach and persuade enough persons in the entire electorate to win a majority of the votes cast.

While it can be argued that the U.S. Constitution provides for a representative form of government, the situation in which the nation found itself 200 years ago is vastly different from that of today.

Most citizens at that early time lived in isolated rural communities with little information regarding either domestic or foreign affairs. Today, the media make such information available in a matter of minutes or hours to virtually the entire population. The typical citizen, therefore, is likely to have access to the same sources of information as a member of Congress.

Highly technical issues cannot be decided by those who are not knowledgeable in such matters, but certainly on nearly all major issues of the day the people collectively are competent to make wise judgments, and the mountain of polling data collected during the last 44 years is proof of this.

One of the early students of the results of refenda held in the state of California was Dr. Max Radin, a member of the law faculty of the University of California. After analyzing some 115 referenda held in that state, Dr. Radin had this to say:

> One thing is clear. The vote of the people is eminently sane. The danger apprehended that quack nostrums in public policy can be forced upon the voters by demagogues is demonstrably non-existent. The representative legislature is much more susceptible to such influences.

Perhaps the best answer comes from Switzerland, which, of all nations of the world, comes nearest to being a pure or direct democracy. In Switzerland people exercise the right of the initiative and the referendum at the local, the cantonal, and the national level. It is not unusual for voters to pass judgment on as many as 50 to 150 issues during the course of a year.

How well has this system of direct democracy worked?

In a poll that we conducted of leaders of the world—persons whose names are listed in the *International Year Book* and *Statesmen's Who's Who*—in which we asked this question: "What nation of the world do you think is best governed?", Switzerland received as many first choices as all other nations of the world combined.

Perhaps, even better evidence comes from the people themselves. When we asked the people in several nations how well satisfied they are with their government, the people of Switzerland expressed the highest level of satisfaction.

The explanation isn't to be found in the fact that Switzerland is a small nation. In theory it should be one of the most difficult nations in the world to govern—with three official languages and two others that are unofficial. The cantons have nurtured their own loyalties and customs over the centuries due largely to the mountain barriers which separate them.

Interestingly, the problem presented by organized minorities is not unique to the United States. The report of a committee on the referendum of the Conservative Party of the United Kingdom had this to say:

> ... We are concerned at the widespread feeling in the country that Parliament is unresponsive to the electorate's views. We should not lightly dismiss the possibility of more effective consultation of the people by government (through the referendum). The case for popular consultations may also be reinforced by the growing complexity and remote-

ness of modern government, as a result of which many people feel alienated from their political institutions and suspicious of the decisions taken through them on their behalf... Governments may need the *explicit support of a popular majority* if they are to secure authority for measures to which *powerful minority interests are opposed...* (Italics are author's.)

A second way to reduce the threat of powerful minorities and to preserve rule of the majority is to adopt reforms that deal with tenure in office and the financing of election campaigns.

The strength of a pressure group lies in the fact that it can help elect or defeat a candidate running for re-election by contributing money and workers to him or to his opponent depending on which will go along with their self-interest legislation. To defeat this carrot-and-stick approach found to be so effective by pressure groups, two reforms are needed. The first would be a limitation on the term of office of senators and members of the House.

We now have a two-term limitation on the office of the presidency and at least two of our former presidents— Truman and Eisenhower—have advocated a two-term limitation on members of the Senate. Eisenhower also supported a 12-year limitation on members of the House.

It could be argued that the very best way to free congressmen to follow their own consciences would be a single term with no re-election. But a two-term limitation at least permits the member of Congress to vote as he sees fit during his last term in office.

The second reform deals with government financing of campaigns. If a candidate did not have to raise a lot of money to carry on his election campaign; if indeed, it were illegal for a candidate to accept money from any individual or any group, then he obviously would be under no obligation to vote as his campaign contributors assume he would, in return for their contribution.

172

When a representative of an American firm offers money or a gift to a member of a foreign business or government hoping to influence that government or firm to buy his product, this is called bribery and is punishable by fine and imprisonment.

When an individual or pressure group gives money to a candidate for office with the tacit understanding that the candidate, if elected, will vote favorably on legislation that benefits the donor, should not this be called by its proper name—bribery?

I have discussed two general approaches which I believe would thwart or lessen the threat of government by well-organized minorities: constitutional amendments to provide for the initiative and referendum, and for limiting the term of office of congressmen. Also, legislation could provide government funding for election campaigns, prohibiting contributions from any other source.

However, I am realistic enough to know that these reforms will be a long time in coming—maybe not in the lifetime of the persons in this audience.

Meanwhile, I believe we should examine our own polling operations to see if we can help bridge the time gap. In short, I believe that we can supply much of the information, through improvement in our polling procedures, that congressmen at present say would be helpful to them.

Specifically, I believe that we can, and should, go much farther than we have in relating knowledge to attitudes. Many years ago, we, at the Gallup Poll developed a question design which enables us to separate the opinions of the informed from those of the uninformed in any area and on any issue. The design permits us to relate different levels of knowledge to attitudes. The design also measures the intensity of feeling about an issue. And we can justly be criticized for not using this design more frequently than we have during the last 30 years.

But our polling task doesn't end here. In addition to

assessing the level of knowledge on a given issue possessed by respondents who are pro or con, we need to identify those who will act on their views—those who care enough about an issue to cast their votes on election day.

If we shed light on these two additional dimensions of public opinion, then we will have largely met the criticism of the congressman who said that he paid little attention to poll findings.

In the early years of polling, we actually thought of substituting the words, "mini-referendum," or "sampling referendum" for the word "poll," largely because polls were associated in the minds of many persons not with public opinion on issues, but with election campaigns and predictions.

There are, in fact, many advantages of a poll over a referendum. Polls can report what all the people think about a given issue—not just those who take the trouble to vote. And polls can identify the groups who favor and those who oppose a given issue with far greated accuracy than is possible by examining election returns. In addition, polls can report the reasons why voters hold the opinions they do.

In conclusion, let me say that polls have an extremely important role to perform in establishing and reporting majority and minority opinion on the important social, economic, and political issues of the day. But they can, and must, go farther than this. They must relate knowledge to attitudes, separating informed from uninformed opinion on complex issues. In addition, they must shed light on the intensity of opinions held, and the likelihood of translating these opinions into action.

Above all, they can help preserve majority rule by poll findings that clearly reveal minority views for exactly what they are—minority views.

Harry W. O'Neill

The Pollster
and the Advocate

BY ADVOCACY RESEARCH I refer to public opinion research conducted for the purpose of providing a client with information to be used in advocating a particular point of view, if, of course, the results of an objective study do in fact support that point of view. Closely related to this type of research is public policy issue research that is conducted for purposes of syndication, general information, or news interest. While this research is not contracted for by an advocate, the same issues often are involved; and the results may well be used subsequently for advocacy purposes.

Some people—both in and out of the survey research profession—raise concerns about the legitimacy of advocacy research with respect to political and public policy issues. These questions include:

Do early, weak poll showings discourage otherwise qualified people from seeking office?

Is it proper for input on a public policy issue from relatively uninformed people to play any role at all in the decision-making process?

Even if well informed, should public opinion affect policy or should policy decisions be made solely by the supposedly reasoned judgment of elected and/or appointed officials?

These are usually posed as rhetorical questions by the critics of political and advocacy research.

Of course, similar critical questions have been raised about other types of survey research. How legitimate is it to engage in marketing and advertising research that is used to exploit the consumer? Or employee research that is used to manipulate the work force? Or corporate image research

that is used to deceive the public? In this manner, the ethical and moral legitimacy of all our endeavors can be challenged.

Advocacy research or public policy issue research, however, is a special case because of the emotional environment usually surrounding the issues involved. This gives rise to another criticism—that is, that it is somehow unprofessional to be involved in research for the express purpose of developing data that may be used to support a particular point of view. And, parenthetically, it is especially unprofessional in the eyes of your critics if your results differ from their preconceptions. Even in the natural sciences, research is not immune to a point of view. Honest scientists can differ in what they think is the relevant evidence. The social sciences are even more subject to such honest differences. Few, if any, of our efforts in the commercial arena are pure research, undertaken only to add to a body of knowledge, and conducted on a plane above day-to-day reality. Quite the contrary, our research efforts—advocacy and otherwise—are undertaken in response to real problems in the real world. There is nothing unprofessional or illegitimate in aiding a particular point of view through public opinion research.

Having said that, I hasten to add that all our research endeavors should be carried out in an objective manner and in accordance with the highest professional standards. And this requirement cannot be over-emphasized with respect to advocacy research. The client for this type of research has a definite point of view. He is not a neutral "seeker of truth." He is not just looking for information to take back to his office and quietly incorporate into some kind of plan of action. He is looking specifically for public opinion data that will strengthen his cause; and he will almost certainly release the results, often with some fanfare, if they support his cause. If the public policy issue research is part of a syndicated service or a news service, the results also will

receive widespread notice. More than in other types of research, therefore, political and public policy issue research faces the possibility of two or more polls on the same issue being released for public view at about the same time. Thus, the reputation of the researcher, the reputation of the researcher's organization, and the reputation of our profession are at stake as in no other kind of survey research. When the various polls are in agreement, we look good. Whatever it is that we do obviously works. But when the various polls differ, we may be in trouble. Even though the differences are understandable within the profession as the result of differing questions or questioning techniques or differing samples or differing points in time, our critics either do not understand these variable or write them off as an excuse rather than an explanation.

It is this public viewing, then, that underscores the need for special care in the conduct of advocacy and public policy issue research—special care with the survey design, the question wording, and the interpretation of the results. Remember, the issues being investigated are emotionally charged and somebody's political or ideological ox will be gored, whatever the results; or somebody's favorite program or pet legislation may well be questioned because of the results. Thus, the risk of aggressive challenge is rather high. And the challenge usually is directed at the question wording. The attacks can come from both the Left and the Right, and there is probably no chance whatsoever that a given set of questions will please everybody. Rest assured that somewhere out there someone is waiting to accuse the advocacy researcher of biased question wording, biased question order, the inclusion of irrelevant issues, the exclusion of relevant issues, oversimplification of issues, or overly complex question wording. And this is understandable. In a science as soft as ours, no survey is ever perfect and, even more important, in the political and public policy issue arena, no one is necessarily going to perceive an issue like anyone else. Hence, from the population of all possible questions that can be asked about an issue, a different selection will be made by different people. The final selection of questions asked in any advocacy poll will be those that, in the eye of the particular researchers working in conjunction with the client, relate to the most important aspects of the issue as they see it.

True, this is a bias, but it is inevitable. Nonetheless, it can and should be minimized. This can best be accomplished by using a team approach to questionnaire construction, in which the team members bring differing viewpoints to the issue under study, and by increasing the scope of the questionnaire to include more aspects of the issue, approach opinion on the issue from a number of directions, and avoid what I call the "Issue in a Vacuum" question—that is, an oversimplified presentation of an issue out of the context of reality. Furthermore, the full disclosure of methodology and question wording, as required by the National Council on Public Polls, the Council of American Survey Research Organizations, and the American Association for Public Opinion Research, should be adhered to without exception. This allows the readers to accept or reject the findings on the basis of their own evaluation of how the survey was conducted.

In addition, caution must be exercised in the interpretation of the results of advocacy and public policy issue research. Results must not be overinterpreted; results must be discussed within the specific context and time frame in which the questions were asked; extrapolation, if any, must be clearly indicated as such.

So with all its problems, its risks, and its potential for controversy, why our involvement with advocacy and public policy issue research? The answer, quite simply, is because such research is in the public interest.

We live in an age of special, or, as they are sometimes

called, public interest groups—one-issue oriented groups—
some of which go to great lengths to make their point of
view known. Not infrequently, they position themselves
either as representing the public's point of view or as
representing what is best for the public. Often they are loud,
activist, and even obstructionist. Hence, they may garner
more than their fair share of public exposure through the
media and exert considerable pressure on elected and appointed officials. Both the public and our officials are
entitled to hear more, are entitled to a more balanced view
of the controversial issues. Special or public interest groups
frequently are nothing more than self-interest groups, often
reflecting minority opinion and taking full advantage of any
lack of opposing views. Thus, not only do all views have a
right to be expressed in public debate; there often is a crying
need for such expression.

Our leaders, in order to govern effectively, and our
candidates, in order to campaign effectively, need to know
where the public stands and which, if any, pressure groups
are in tune with the mood of the country. This is a large,
diverse country trying to function in a democratic manner.
Advocacy and public policy issue research play an important role in this process, since research provides a
representative point of view unlike that obtained in any
other way. This is not to suggest that our leaders should not
lead. After all, one function of a leader is to mold public
opinion, to lead the public, away from what might be short-
sighted, self-centered, short-term approaches to a problem
and toward accepting an approach that is more in the
nation's long-term interest. This process can be more effective, however, if the leadership has an accurate understanding of where and why the public stands on the problem or
issue in question. Sound research can indicate how far the
public has to be moved, the nature of the obstacles to be
overcome, the arguments that stand the best chance of
changing public opinion. On the other hand, there are issues

on which current public opinion should be taken into account more directly—issues on which it is better that the public be served than a self-serving official be satisfied.

The key questions for those who are exposed to the results of advocacy and public policy issue research are these:

When is it appropriate to pay attention to the polls?

How much importance should be given to public opinion as expressed in the polls?

The answer to the first is easy. It is always appropriate to pay attention to the polls because that is akin to listening to the voice of the public—a requirement, in my opinion, for the survival of democracy. How much weight should be given to the polls is, indeed, a much more difficult question to which there is no definitive answer. Strategic foreign policy decisions, for example, need not be concerned with public opinion, except in very exceptional instances. However, once a foreign policy decision is made, if it is at variance with the public view as expressed in the polls, then the decision-makers should publicly acknowledge this variance and present their rationale for the decision. This recognizes the importance of public opinion in a democracy even when it is inappropriate to incorporate that opinion into the decision-making process. At the other end of the scale, the decision by a city council as to whether or not to build a community swimming pool might well be made solely on the basis of a public opinion poll. In between the extremes of the examples given are many shades of gray. For each situation the role of public opinion must be individually determined on the basis of the issue itself, as well as some evaluation of the stage of public opinion on the issue—that is, has the public formed its mature opinion or is opinion in an early, formative period?

This last matter, of course, points to the need for trend studies to track public opinion, to determine whether it has crystallized or whether it is still undergoing change. More important for deciding how much importance should be given to public opinion as expressed in polls is the particular poll itself. As you should know, there are good polls and there is junk that masquerades as good research. Although there is ever-increasing exposure to and interest in poll results, there has by no means been a commensurate increase in the understanding of what is and is not an acceptable survey. Unfortunately, almost anything called a "poll" receives uncritical acceptance by advocates and the media if the percentages suit their cause or spark their interest. Too few people know how to or take the time to differentiate a sound polling effort from the quick-and-dirty asking of a few ill-conceived questions of an unscientifically chosen bunch of people for a questionable motive.

While any special interest or any medium has a legitimate right to commission a public opinion survey and an equally legitimate right to use the results in its advocacy or informational activities, it is our responsibility as survey research professionals to be associated with only sound research endeavors and to ensure that the results of these endeavors are used in a responsible manner. Surveys of this type will be held up for scrutiny and they must be able to pass the test or we destroy our credibility across the board—with those who would be our clients, with those who should attend to our results, and with the public who must be our respondents. Let me give but one very recent example. Writing critically about an NBC/AP poll on SALT II in the October issue of the *Washington Monthly,* Charles Peters said: "National polls cost a lot of money and the less questions asked the lower the cost. Networks don't want long, complicated stories anyway. So a desire for brevity combines with a desire to hold down costs to produce public opinion that is not public opinion at all."

We must be firm in dealing with those who would commission advocacy, public policy issue, or political research.

POLLING ON THE ISSUES

We can accept no shortcuts in design, no bias in the questions, no omission of relevant items to shorten the questionnaire for fear of the outcome. We must provide an interpretation of the results. We must allow no selective or otherwise misleading use of the results. It is our responsibility to establish the guidelines for both the research and the release of findings; and if they are not acceptable to our client, we should refuse the assignment; or, if the results are used in an unethical or inaccurate manner, we have an obligation to take whatever steps are necessary to correct the situation. Working through our professional associations, we must educate those who use research results, enforce proper standards, and bring to public view those who violate the canons of objective research. And we must always keep in mind that in our professional role we are neutral suppliers of information, not partisans or advocates ourselves.

The role of advocacy and public policy issue research in the world of business, government, and politics is growing, and rightly so. This type of research, however, will always have its critics. It is our challenge to give them little to criticize, but never to allow them to deter us from our investigations of the important political and social issues of the day.

Mervin D. Field

Public Polls
and the Public Interest

IN OUR POLITICAL and social system, a wide variety of
individuals and institutions act as brokers between the
public and decision-makers. Some of these brokers include
media owners and media spokespersons, elected leaders,
self-appointed leaders of social institutions and groups,
economists, financial experts, the physical science author-
ities, and public personalities who represent various causes.
In recent years, public opinion pollsters have joined the
ranks of political and social process brokers and, because
the structure of polling involves a systematic if not scientific
procedure, a special aura of objectivity and importance is
assigned to polls and pollsters.

It is generally recognized that to the extent the communications industry, business, government, or a special interest
group acquires information about the public mind, it acquires a kind of power which enables it to manipulate or
take advantage of the public either directly or indirectly.
This manipulation may take the form of concealing poll
information, making selective leaks of the information, or
issuing data which are faulty or biased. Apart from this kind
of manipulation, there is the problem of people assuming
that public opinion on a policy issue has been definitively
described when the results of a poll on the subject have been
reported. We all know that in many cases, all that's been
heard is the public's answers to selected questions put to a
sample of the public by a research agency or a special
interest group. Only rarely does anyone's study ever explore
all of the valid alternatives on issues.

Nonetheless, there is still an aura of infallibility associated with any kind of poll data. As a society which puts an

inordinate value on impeccable arithmetic, we always feel comfortable about something which adds up to 100 percent. Although the 100 percent total will occur with answers to even the most cockeyed questions, the impression of certainty conveyed unfortunately inhibits close scrutiny of question wording and sampling methodology.

I think more attention needs to be given to the circumstances under which policy research should be conducted. Many policy research studies today are undertaken on issues to which the public has given little thought; often the basic issue that is under study is obscure and the public's interest or accumulated knowledge is meager. One of the long-standing criticisms of opinion research, which unfortunately has considerable validity, is that large portions of the public are not ready to respond to some of our most serious and political questions—particularly when they are being polled mainly to satisfy some narrow journalistic or policy-interest goal for a poll sponsor who has a particular set agenda. We know that large portions of the public are not really informed enough to respond meaningfully to some of the most serious social and political questions. There is unfortunately some truth to Oscar Wilde's contemptuous definition that "public opinion is simply an invention which takes community ignorance and elevates it to the level of a political force."

Democracy has always been faced with the dilemma of how much weight should be given to the opinions of a relatively unknowledgeable public in the setting of public policy. We know that many policymakers will be unduly influenced by a public opinion study which purports to show the will of the people but which, in fact, is merely a whim of the people based on their disinterest and incomplete understanding of an issue. On the other side of the coin, in the absence of actual knowledge of public opinion, policymakers find themselves increasingly dependent on self-appointed representatives of the public. It's not always clear what positions these people are representing—what the public wants, what it should want, or what it should be permitted to want.

We pollsters too often ask the public for opinions where none may exist. In developing and testing our questionnaires, we may find that only a small fraction of the public is aware of an issue, but this does not stop us from asking the entire sample its opinion on the issue. Respondents can be baffled because they cannot relate to the questions that we pose. In effect, if we ask a question in terms unfamiliar to a respondent, there is no "answer space" in their heads that fits the way the question is asked. One example we can all recall is the childhood trauma of being compelled to answer such questions as "What are you doing here without your sweater?" As adults many of us still feel obliged to give some kind of answer.

Many of us have succumbed to the exercise of being very adroit at asking our sample long lists of sophisticated questions. The hope is that even if a respondent is ignorant of an issue, we might be able to tap some latent disposition. So we press on with questions which "educate" the respondent on the spot to pro and con arguments about the issue. Many of us recognize that once we are in the position of "educating" the respondent to the pros and cons of an issue we are on dangerous ground. We try to be objective and to pose balanced arguments, but how can we be sure?

Posing arguments pro and con in the question preamble may be an honest attempt to bring a respondent up to speed, so to speak, but it is grandiose to think that we can simulate all that happens in the normal course of information intake. That involves source credibility, interest level, complexity, repetition of arguments, and knowledge of events or facts, to name just a few aspects which relate to settled opinion judgment.

Often in these instances, all that we have done is a fairly superficial job of educating a small group of respondents.

We have done so in the mistaken and perhaps honest belief that in the interview situation we can simulate the process which results from attending to the policy issue debate as presented by the media and by the leadership or, experiencing an educating effect from the normal discourse and observation of daily activities. I am afraid that the further we go on this path, the further we get away from the real opinion and attitude measurement and the worthwhile utility of our findings. At best, some of these clever, razzle-dazzle questionnaire exercises are simply esoteric laboratory experiments which rarely are replicated in real life.

Another source of danger in public policy polling is that too much objectivity is imputed to some policy researchers who are also researchers for political candidates or are otherwise involved in political decision-making. These researchers not only produce data but interpret and implement them as well. While a few persons may be capable of performing this delicate balancing act, I think most humans are not. Good research methodologists are not necessarily good policymakers and vice versa. Describing well is not necessarily deciding well.

During a campaign, private pollsters are called upon to advise candidates how to win. This entails identifying with the candidates and being subjective about campaign events. I have long felt uncomfortable about the conflict of interest that results when a political pollster offers advice on how to use survey results on behalf of a candidate or a cause. I know of many distressing examples of pollsters failing to do justice to one or the other of their disparate roles. Political campaigns are intense pressure cookers. A person who is both a reseacher and a counselor during a political campaign usually finds the research component of this hybrid combination the first to be impaired.

I feel very uneasy when I see reports by these same pollsters on public policy issues. Are they providing really objective reports or are they deliberately or inadvertently influenced by the positions of some of their political clients? When a private pollster declares his bias by choosing to work only for candidates or causes of one type, it may seem to enhance his image for personal integrity, but it makes me wonder how professional and objective the pollster really can be.

All pollsters must recognize that their findings are often likely to be the subject of controversy. Even qualified conclusions based on highly sophisticated analysis can be controversial. Simply because there is controversy, or even attack, does not imply that the conclusions are necessarily wrong. Controversies over methods and findings should be expected, welcomed, and valued as assets in the progress of research. Truly scientific controversies are potentially resolvable by the addition of new hypotheses and facts. This can only take place when researchers make full disclosure of their methods and results. This permits additional research to be performed as a kind of rival replication to confirm or disprove a study's findings and conclusions.

In recent years, professional pollsters and researchers have set laudable standards for disclosing survey methodological information which are absolutely essential in the efforts of the industry to promote responsible conduct. Unfortunately, in an excess of zeal to be more responsible in conveying poll data, many media people seem to have fixed on the statistical tolerance apparent in survey findings as the key factor, completely neglecting other important determinants of the validity and reliability of the poll data.

For example, we see TV network anchor people and news reporters showing that 65 percent of Americans support the SALT II treaty and then adding that this finding has a tolerance of 4 percentage points, plus or minus. This leaves the public with the impression that the outer limits of the true figure are 61 percent and 69 percent. I submit that this is a classic example of misleading precision. We all know that survey data contain the probability of a number of significant non-random errors, any of which could produce a numerical variance many times larger than the sampling variance. Consequently, the purveyor of the findings, with perhaps the best of intentions, drags a red herring across the trail, lulling most of the public into a sense of security about the data which may be illusory.

Polling and public opinion research in the political and public policy areas is now so large and important an activity that it requires more scrutiny than it now is receiving. One way that this might be accomplished is through the development of more professional research critics and evaluators, persons well-grounded in survey methodology whose primary efforts are devoted to evaluating public policy research. I think they could provide a corrective bias against the problems posed by improperly evaluated advocacy research and the uncritical acceptance of potentially invalid information as a basis for public policy.

Parallel roles exist in other fields. Financial reports get close scrutiny and evaluation from security analysts. New books, plays, and movies get thorough critical attention from people whose job it is to know and understand the author's meaning. Investigative reporters and political analysts pride themselves on knowing how to separate the wheat from the chaff of material coming from government officials, corporate spokesmen, and other sources. I think that a similar discipline could arise and flourish in the field of public policy research and poll reports.

Working researchers should also not be reticent about discussing or criticizing other researchers' efforts. We have encountered some such criticism in these discussions, and I think it's most refreshing. It is rare, however, to see any public criticism from within the profession. No doubt this results from the code of professional courtesy, or from a natural fear that your own efforts may come under unflattering retaliatory review. Still, there needs to be more protection for peer review within the profession.

A Political Institution?

Public opinion researchers owe a huge debt to social science and to the public from which they derive their data. I believe that for the right to use the tools and concepts of scientific methods and the cooperation of the thousands of people who give their time to participate in surveys and to maximize the benefits of that marvelous tool, the question-naire survey, pollsters should not only welcome but take the lead in assuring more critical scrutiny of their efforts.

Floor
Discussion

DAVID H. WEAVER*: I don't really disagree about the extent to which reporting sampling error can be misleading, but I personally would be against telling journalists, "Don't report it at all." It does give people an idea that some error must be accounted for in sampling and, of course, we all know there are other sources of possible error. What advice would you give a journalist?

MERVIN FIELD: I would say that pollsters should disclose to their sponsors all the qualifications inherent in the data and that the sponsors, particularly media sponsors, should then make decisions about what needs to be reported. If the media report is two minutes of air time or less, I think a mention of sampling error can be misleading. It is really a matter of degree. Some of the more responsible papers and broadcasters are devoting more time and space to explaining the components of possible error. The *New York Times,* for example, often gives three big columns to the data and then a small box at the end of the story describing methodology. I think they ought to enlarge that box and qualify the survey findings adequately. Either you have to explain the potential sources of error thoroughly, or not at all.

SHELDON R. GAWISER**: I think we all agree that it would be lovely to have a more extensive statement about error margins and about the components of error in a survey, both in TV news and in the papers also; but I have two

---

* Professor of Journalism and Director of the Bureau of Media Research, Indiana University.
** Senior Survey Director, National Opinion Research Center.

questions. Do you think the listening audience senses less precision if there is no statement of error at all than if the error margin statement is made? Secondly, what kind of statement do you make in your surveys that explains this? Is there a statement you make that you feel gives an indication of the other sources of error?

MERVIN FIELD: The public has been exposed to poll data for a generation. The more sophisticated know that different polls get different results. But when Walter Cronkite or another authoritative figure reports a tolerance, it is misleading. It would be better not to report it. With regard to your second question, we have been trying to evolve a statement about possible error. Typically we have a three-page release with data, to which we add a fourth page. On one side we give all the data to comply with the codes of the National Council on Public Polls and the American Association for Public Opinion Research in such areas as sample size, weighting, and the disclosure of questions not already included in the release. On the back of that page we have a long statement explaining what goes into survey accuracy. We do have a box which is still not satisfactory in which we say that sampling tolerance is one factor, but that in addition there could be minor error because we could ask the question differently and get a different response. I must say that editors aren't using that much, but we find they are becoming more receptive to it.

WARREN J. MITOFSKY: Since I am a minority in this crowd, I feel somewhat responsible for Walter Cronkite's statements. I would like to suggest that what you are saying is totally irresponsible! We all know that every number in any survey has a sampling error and that three percent is a generalization. If we talk about Republicans, who are perhaps 20 percent in a sample of 1,500, we know the sampling error is somewhat larger. If we were a survey with a sample size of 400 in the newspaper, we know the sampling error is larger than it is for a sample of 1,500. Granted that the sampling error is not the only kind of possible error, I have never heard any of the people who propose that we *not* state sampling error indicate what we should say about the magnitude of the possible error. I've never had any guidance on how you analyze data given the limitations introduced by other kinds of error. Sampling error does at least put the findings into some limited context. It is not an absolute answer to the data analysis problem. It is just an indication of one limitation in the data. You cannot withhold knowledge of sampling error by saying there are other errors. It is a disservice not to inform your reader, or your viewer, that there is a known and measurable source of error.

BURNS ROPER: I do not think you can publish a book on television or even in the *New York Times* that would explain all the possible sources of error. A much better clue for the reader or the listener about the source of error is to give the question asked and not mention the "plus or minus three percentage points." If the question is given, the reader or viewer can make a judgment as to what the possible error is.

BARRY SUSSMAN: I think there is another way to address this problem. Since most of the questions arise when you deal with percentages (*e.g.,* 60/40, 52/48) and since we are talking primarily about reporting results to the public, I agree wholeheartedly that you ought to give the wording of the question. To the extent possible, you ought to look for and report gross differences. That is, if there is a narrow split on a question, you ought to report that it is a narrow split, rather than a specific figure. When it comes to the president's popularity rating, then we become stuck with a figure, for example a 33 percent approval rating. Or in an election trial heat, in which the focus is on "the way the election would turn out if it were being held today." If you do have a close split in an election trial heat, and you're reporting it in a newspaper, it would be better not to focus on the narrow percentages or the margin of error, but rather on how the people you interviewed break into blocs—who's for and who's against—and occasionally tell the reader about margin of error and thus why you are nervous about the close split.

JEFFREY MILSTEIN*: I'd like to turn to something else for a minute. I know that people are concerned about the cost of doing polls and I know the cost is roughly $1 per person per minute for a telephone survey. Doubling your sample size costs more money but, when you think about it, you can do a lot more robust research for the same amount of money by not being so concerned about sampling error and sample size, and instead try a different approach. For example, by lengthening your questionnaire, you can ask a question in different ways to get at a range on the attitude that you are trying to measure. Or, you can take totally different samples, perhaps even small samples of 100, and ask a different series of questions. Or, you can focus on measuring behavior, rather than opinions. All of these approaches can be pursued within the same research budget. Then you are in a position to take those different pieces of information and arrive at an estimate, not to enable you to say 52.3 percent think this way, but to be able to conclude that, measured in many different ways, roughly half of the public feels so and so. We would be more confident of this kind of a finding because it had emerged from many different kinds of measures.

ALBERT H. CANTRIL: I would like to ask a question of three individuals in the audience: Bernard Roshco, Jeffrey Milstein, and Daniel Melnick. A conference on "polling on

---

* Office of Conservation and Solar Energy, Department of Energy.

the issues" raises the very real question of how decision makers have poll material provided to them. Each of these individuals is involved in providing a different kind of staffing support as regards poll findings. Bernard Roshco works in the Bureau of Public Affairs of the Department of State. Given constraints on the Department's ability to commission surveys, Roshco and his colleagues rely primarily on the syndicated polls and media polls for their data, supplement them with some secondary analysis, and keep track of trends by referring to their archive of opinion data on foreign policy topics. Jeffrey Milstein is in a different position and is able to commission surveys for the Department of Energy. Dan Melnick works for the Congressional Research Service, a third kind of setting in which characteristically there are multiple research inquiries under way at the same time. The question I'd like each to address is how do you try to get meaningful opinion data to your principals?

BERNARD ROSHCO*: The paper on SALT by William Lanouette illustrates what we have to do, and our difficulties in doing it. Polls often are useful to us to the extent that they display contradictions in public opinion. There is nothing more dangerous to a policymaker than only one set of results on a complex issue such as SALT. In the spring of 1979, Barry Sussman tried to do a SALT poll without talking about SALT. It was interesting because he tried to ask questions that would evoke the attitudes that seemed to be playing a role in shaping public reaction to SALT. And that's a significant part of what we do—try to find out what shapes the public's views on an issue. For us, one of the utilities of poll material, at a fairly complicated level and with lots of contradictions in it, is that it illustrates the cross-currents of public reaction. We try to make the people inside the State Department see the issue not in the

---

* Senior Public Opinion Analyst, Department of State.

very specialized terms that they deal with, but as the public outside sees it. Several problems, however, dog our efforts. Most often we face a severe lack of questions about how much the public knows about an issue. For example, there was only one knowledge question on the Panama Canal issue. So, we never really learned how many people knew who owned the Panama Canal. Secondly, we often do not know how intensely opinion is held. While we have found more knowledge questions on SALT, the research to date has been peculiarly lacking in questions that measure the intensity of feeling. So you see, we are dependent on the needs, biases and desires of pollsters—some of whom are polling for advocacy purposes and some of whom are polling for 90-second news stories. We try to do the best we can with what we get.

DANIEL MELNICK*: We work for about 800 bosses in the sense that we provide support to 800 congressional offices—individual senators, congressmen, and various committee staffs. Our role is a bit different from that described by Bernard Roshco at the Department of State in that basically we try to locate the results of surveys from all points of view which are pertinent to the concerns of requests from congressional offices. Sometimes that involves analysis of poll data; sometimes it involves providing offices with information about the methods of polling. We try to present them with as balanced a view of the results as we can. That is to say, we try to give them everything we have that uses reasonable survey procedures. We provide policy analysis, but we shy away from providing any policy recommendations. The Congressional Research Service has been engaged in a massive process of attempting to find as many surveys as possible, using newspaper clippings and other sources. We have a very broad level of

---

*Specialist in American National Government (Public Opinion Survey Research), Congressional Research Service.

cooperation from a large number of organizations that provide us with information on a regular basis. We seek to get more information this way. In terms of poll disclosure, I have never been in a situation with any survey service or organization where we requested methodological information we didn't receive. On occasion, organizations have been restrained from providing us with complete questionnaires but we understand that some of the questions are proprietary.

JEFFREY MILSTEIN: Over the past five and a half years, I have directed more than 25 national surveys for the Department of Energy. In recent years, we have also looked to the results of the polls in the media or released by organizations. Pollsters provide a service to the public at large as well as to policymakers at all levels of government. Because energy is of such importance to the whole nation, it would help sharpen the issues debated if the quality of polls on energy could be improved. Very often, for example, we find closed-ended questions when we could get more valuable information by asking people the simple question, "What is your definition of the energy problem?"* When you ask the question in an open-ended form, your whole view of public attitudes is very different from the picture gained from narrrowly defined, forced-choice questions. Secondly, in reviewing the polls and reporting on them, I would urge a greater effort to look at the kinds of trade-offs people are willing to make. Everybody's for conservation, solar energy, and clean air; but everybody also wants plenty of electricity. We ought to be framing questions in terms of these real world trade-offs. Questions are often superficial, missing the underlying values at work. We could get better readings on values about growth, materialism, faith in

---

* A "closed-ended question" is one in which response alternatives are specified in the question; an "open-ended question" is one that invites a free response that is recorded verbatim by the interviewer.

technology, cynicism about the political and social structure, and, of course, about the extent of public understanding and knowledge on an issue. The fact that only one
person in ten knows even vaguely how much energy we
import is important. I commented earlier on the need to get
better readings on behavior: How many people are car-
pooling? Insulating their homes? Buying more efficient
cars? It is easier and probably more valid to get at the
behavioral dimensions, rather than exclusively at attitudes
or opinion. It would be useful to get rolling panels so that
when a quarter or a third of your original sample is
reinterviewed, you can see individual change. Often the
change from one poll to the next will be swamped by
sampling error. Finally, it would be useful to frame questions in such a way that people aren't given the wrong
concept of what we are really talking about. In energy
conservation, for example, we talk about energy efficiency,
but often the questions are so framed in terms of sacrifice.
Nobody wants to sacrifice. And that is not really the issue as
we become a more energy-efficient country. In terms of
obtaining data, we are eager to have access to whatever
reports polling organizations issue and to the raw data, for
further analysis. In turn, the Department of Energy has
contributed data from polls it has commissioned to the
archives at the Inter-University Consortium for Political
Research at Ann Arbor, Michigan.

ALBERT H. CANTRIL: As we bring the conference to a close,
let me assert the prerogative of the chair to make a couple of
comments. We have heard a diversity of points of view
expressed today on critical issues within the field of public
opinion research and regarding its relationship to the
decision-making community. If I carry away any overall
impression of the discussion it is the fairly general consensus
that the public opinion poll has the capacity for the precise
measurement of public sentiment but that it is a tool that we

use bluntly all too often. For reasons of convention within the profession as well as pressures operating on it from outside, pollsters persist in a preoccupation with producing that single number—percentage of the public—that must somehow bear the burden of conveying the state of opinion on an issue, no matter how complex it is or how riddled with contradictions public opinion may be. But I do not despair. There was ample testimony today that we pollsters are increasingly sensitive to the problem. So, too, are journalists who report our findings and those at the policy level of government. To the extent that the conference helped sharpen our concern in this regard, it will have made a contribution.

National Council On Public Polls

Members

American Institute of Public Opinion (Gallup Poll)
Bureau of Social Science Research
Cantril Research, Inc.
CBS NEWS
Des Moines Register and Tribune (Iowa Poll)
Elections Research Center
The Field Institute (California Poll)
GMA Research Corporation
Louis Harris and Associates
Peter D. Hart Research Associates
National Opinion Research Center
Opinion Research Corporation
Polls, Inc.
Response Analysis Corporation
The Roper Organization
Yankelovich, Skelly and White

Principles of Disclosure

We, the member organizations of the National Council on Public Polls, hereby affirm our commitment to standards of disclosure designed to insure that consumers of survey results that enter the public domain have an adequate basis for judging the reliability and validity of the results reported.

It shall not be the purpose of this Code to pass judgment on the merits of methods employed in specific surveys. Rather, it shall be our sole purpose to insure that pertinent information is disclosed concerning methods that were used so that consumers of surveys may assess studies for themselves.

Any survey organization, upon providing evidence to the Council of its compliance with this Code, shall be permitted to state that it "complies with the Principles of Disclosure of the National Council on Public Polls."

To the above ends, we agree with the following Principles of Disclosure and procedures to be followed in the event question is raised about compliance with them.

Principles

All reports of survey findings of member organizations, prepared specifically for public release, will include reference to the following:

- Sponsorship of the survey;
- Dates of interviewing;
- Method of obtaining the interviews (in-person, telephone or mail);
- Population that was sampled;
- Size of the sample;
- Size and description of the sub-sample, if the survey report relies primarily on less than the total sample;
- Complete wording of questions upon which the release is based; and,
- The percentages upon which conclusions are based.

When survey results are released to any medium by a survey organization, the above items will be included in the release and a copy of the release will be filed with the Council within two weeks.

Survey organizations reporting results will endeavor to have print and broadcast media include the above items in their news stories and make a report containing these items available to the public upon request.

Organizations conducting privately commissioned surveys should make clear to their clients that the client has the right to maintain the confidentiality of survey findings. However, in the event results of a privately commissioned poll are made public by the survey organization, it shall be assumed that they have entered the public domain and the above eight items should be disclosed. In the event the results of a privately commissioned poll are made public by the client and the client acknowledges the release, the survey organization (a) shall make the information outlined above available to the public upon request and (b) shall have the responsibility to release the information above and other pertinent information necessary to put the client's release into the proper context if such a release has misrepresented the survey's findings.

Procedure

It is reasonable to require disclosure of pertinent information regarding methods when questions are raised about survey results or how a survey has been conducted. The purpose of such disclosure will be to insure that adequate information is available, not to evaluate the specific techniques that were employed.

Accordingly, the procedures outlined below will be used when question is raised:

a. Whether a member organization has complied with the Principles of Disclosure; or
b. Regarding the methods employed in a survey by a member organization and the complaining party has not been able to obtain the desired information directly.

These procedures are designed to insure due process:

1. The President will make available a copy of the complaint to the member organization involved, including the identity of the individual or organization bringing the complaint.
2. The Committee on Disclosure will consider the matter and determine whether or not the question is of sufficient significance to warrant fuller disclosure of methods employed.
3. If two-thirds of a quorum of the Committee feel the question is sufficiently important, the matter will be pursued as described below. Otherwise, the matter will be dropped.

   a. The Committee on disclosure will determine (by two-thirds vote of a quorum) within one month which aspects of methodology shall be required to

201

be disclosed, including, but not limited to, any or all of the following:

- Sample design: sampling frame, stages, number of sampling points, clustering, respondent selection, number of callbacks, refusal rate, substitution rules (if any) and non-contract rate of sample units;
- Sample composition: weighted and unweighted demographics for the sample upon which reported results are based (including sub-samples if reports are based upon less than the total sample);
- Questions preceding the question or questions upon which reported results are based that may bias the pattern of response;
- All filter questions that were used when results of a partial sample are reported;
- Weighting procedures which bear upon the derivation of reported results; and
- Sampling error.

b. Within two weeks of a decision by the Committee on Disclosure, the member organization will be notified by the Chairman of the Committee about which methodological aspects the Committee feels information should be disclosed.

c. The member organization shall then have two weeks to make the information available to the Committee on Disclosure without prejudice or to indicate why it feels it cannot provide the requested information.

d. In the event the member organization does not provide the requested information to the Committee on Disclosure within the two-week period, the Chairman will report to the President of the Council, who will in turn advise the full Council of the impasse by presenting (a) the question raised initially, (b) the request for information of the Committee on Disclosure, and (c) the reply of the member organization.

e. The matter will then be put to a vote of the full Council, which can by majority vote decide that the member organization can be placed on probation for a specified period of time or even expelled from the Council. In either case, the member organization shall be precluded from stating that its surveys comply with the Principles of Disclosure of the Council, unless and until it is restored to good standing.

f. In the event the Committee on Disclosure determines that the question raised is significant enough to proceed as outlined in this protocol, the record of the actions of the Committee and the response of the member organization shall be made public through publication in a relevant publication.

g. In the event that a party to a disagreement feels due process has not been followed, two courses of action may be taken: (a) the entire matter shall be turned over to the American Arbitration Association and all parties agree that its determination shall be binding, including its allocation of any expenses that may be incurred; or (b) the entire matter shall be discussed at a hearing called for the purposes of informing the organization why sanctions have been recommended and giving the organization the opportunity to defend its position of non-compliance to the membership of the Council with a complete record of such hearing kept and made available to the public upon request.

Adopted: September 1979

Index

206

Acknowledgments

This volume has grown out of the labors of many individuals, from the planning of the Conference to the publication of its proceedings. In particular, attention should be called to Charles L. Willis of the Kettering Foundation. He was a genuine colleague in all phases of the project. His support and judgment were essential to the success of the effort. We also have valued the encouragement of Phillips B. Ruopp.

Susan Davis Cantril collaborated in the planning and conduct of the Conference and, in effect, served as co-editor of this volume.

Both before and during the Conference itself, Carol Farquhar handled many of the organizational responsibilities with skill and good humor. We wish to express our appreciation to Barry Sussman and the *Washington Post* for providing an ideal conference setting.

With respect to this publication, we are indebted to Robert Daley and Calvin Kytle. Carole Jacobs lent a strong editorial hand.

A.H.C.